Seven Contemporary Chinese Women Writers

Panda Books

Panda Books
First edition 1982
Second printing 1983
Third printing 1985
Copyright 1982 by CHINESE LITERATURE
ISBN 0-8351-1600-x

Published by Chinese Literature, Beijing (37), China
Distributed by China International Book Trading Corporation
(GUOJI SHUDIAN) P.O. Box 399, Beijing
Printed in the People's Republic of China

CONTENTS

Preface

"WOMEN scientists and writers are few in our country," states Huang Zongying in "The Flight of the Wildgeese". True, compared with men they are few, but their number is growing. There are 220 women in the Writers' Association who, while drawing regular salaries from the editorial board, film studio or writers' association to which they are attached, spend most of their time on creative work. In this volume we introduce seven representative women writers, whose stories and reportage present a good cross-section of life in China.

Although the writers selected vary considerably in age, experience and background, all show a strong sense of social responsibility. In China, literature is not viewed as a form of entertainment or simply as a source of aesthetic enjoyment, but as an effective means of education, of inspiring readers with high ideals and the belief that these can be attained. This revolutionary idealism is a feature of all seven pieces presented here.

At the same time these stories reflect reality. China's relaxed political climate and growing democracy in the last few years have resulted in more truthful writing and a wider range of themes. Love, social injustice, the value of the individual, humanism and other subjects formerly taboo are now being fearlessly tackled — often with an unabashed display of emotion. Social

problems dating from or arising after the "cultural revolution" are the themes chosen by most women writers.

However, one problem not dealt with explicitly is
that of the status of women in China today. There is
no militant writing about the issue of women's eman-
cipation. According to the constitution, women and
men have equal rights in China; but this cannot be fully
carried out in practice yet, although the position of
women is now vastly improved. These stories tell us
indirectly a good deal about their status.

It is significant that the heroines of "At Middle Age"
and "The Flight of the Wild-geese" are skilled professionals, the surgeon Dr Lu and the botanist Qin. After
the founding of the People's Republic intellectuals were
seldom cast in leading roles in literature, for emphasis
was placed on presenting workers and peasants as the
heroes of our times. Lu and Qin are devoted to their
work and serve the people with great technical skill,
but neither receives official recognition for her contribution. Indeed Qin is under a cloud because she has
been labelled as a landlord's daughter and has of-
fended certain bureaucrats. Her Party secretary, who
should have a high ideological level and give political
guidance, makes the revealing male-chauvinist remark,
"Although she has her faults, we must make allowances
for her being a woman."

Dr Lu works overtime in the hospital and at home
bears the brunt of housework and minding the children,
yet feels guiltily that she is a bad wife and mother.
Many Chinese professional women have this sense of
guilt. All women, even those with small children,
work after their 56-day maternity leave. In a materially backward country like this, there are few labour-

saving devices, housework is wearisome and time-consuming, and in the cities people often spend hours queuing up to buy vegetables. Many women age prematurely trying to be good housewives while at the same time improving their technical skills. Zhang Jie has said to me on several occasions, "To be a woman is hard!" But there is no women's liberation movement in China, partly because women's position is infinitely better than before, partly because they see their problems in the general social context and are working for modernization to lighten their burdens. This explains why their difficulties are presented as something peripheral, not as the central theme of most of these stories.

What concerns our women writers most is the younger generation. Zong Pu describes the generation gap between certain old intellectuals attacked during the ten years of chaos and the younger generation who suffered on account of their parents. These young people seem cynical, flippant, materialistic, but they have their ideals too. "Melody in Dreams" shows some of them risking arrest by denouncing the feudal fascism of the "gang of four" during the Tiananmen Incident in 1976, and scoffing at their elders who urge them to play safe.

Other problems of young people are frankly presented: their disrupted education; lack of interesting employment; the difficulties met with by boys and girls sent from town to the countryside; the low incomes and overcrowding which threaten to break up young couples' marriages; their mental confusion after the turbulent years in which revolutionary traditions were thrown overboard and bureaucracy, nepotism and corruption were rampant.... Women writers are truthful spokesmen for the youth. If they have not experienced for themselves the problems of the young, they do their homework conscientiously. Thus before writing "The Path Through the Grassland" Ru Zhijuan went to live for a period in the Daqing oilfield.

Shen Rong, before writing "At Middle Age" about the difficulties of middle-aged intellectuals, familiarized herself with a hospital in Beijing. Embarking on a story like this took courage, because there is still some uncertainty about the dividing line between positive exposure of problems and abuses and anti-socialist writing. This work aroused attention to problems for which there can be no rapid solution — how to improve the material conditions of overworked professionals.

Courage of the same kind is shown in Huang Zongying's sensitive reportage "The Flight of the Wildgeese". The woman botanist Qin has the same high sense of responsibility, professional expertise and idealism as Dr Lu. But for years she has been considered politically backward. A reporter following up her case to establish the truth might well offend the higher authorities.

Zhang Jie's "Love Must Not Be Forgotten" aroused considerable interest as well as much controversy. It has been included in this selection because she considers it one of her most representative works. Boldly unconventional, idealistic and intensely romantic, it sheds interesting light on the changes in the attitude to love in socialist China, still strongly influenced by feudal ideas about marriage.

Many of the stories here stress human sympathy or love and friendship even during sharp class struggles. This is a positive feature following a period during which relations between individuals were affected by the current political line — a man in trouble might be divorced by his wife and repudiated by his children, even if they believed that he had done nothing wrong. The botanist Qin, for example, is not a black or white stereotype, but a complex human being, principled and dedicated to serving the people, yet over-sensitive and liable to lose her temper. Although she is labelled as the daughter of a landlord, the mountain villagers love her for her concern for them and her selfless work to improve their livelihood.

The ultra-Left line in literature in the past encouraged writing according to set formulas, and the ten years of turmoil deprived young would-be writers of a good education and the access to classical Chinese and foreign literature needed to raise the quality of their work. This is evident from the immaturity, lack of sophistication and verbosity of certain stories. But the last few years have been a period of experimentation in finding fresher forms and styles, and women writers are paying attention to this. However, their works are above all significant because of their subject matter and the honest picture they present of life in China today.

Gladys Yang

Ru Zhijuan in 1979

Ru Zhijuan

RU Zhijuan, born in Shanghai in 1925, lost her mother when still a small child. Brought up by her grandmother, she was forced by poverty to leave primary school after only four years of study.

In 1943 she joined a theatrical troupe in the New Fourth Army and carried out propaganda at the front. In '50 she published her first short story. In '55 she became a member of the Chinese Writers' Association and helped to edit *Literary Monthly*. Many of the earlier themes of her stories were drawn from the War of Liberation, but she now writes on a wide range of subjects. Her stories are well constructed, felicitously written, and the characters' psychology is subtly conveyed. A council member of the Chinese Writers' Association, she is now on the editorial board of *Shanghai Literature*.

The Path Through the Grassland

Ru Zhijuan

THE desolate grassland stretched out as if to the end of the world. On a piece of uncultivated land as vast as this, one could have made straight for anywhere, but the narrow path running across it was zigzag and winding. It must have been trodden out by people who, enchanted by this scene, stared this way and that, not knowing where to go, or strolled along absent-mindedly, lost in thought. Yet, no matter how the track twisted, it was bound to lead somewhere.

Just off her night shift, Xiao Tai had got a sample from Well 48. This well was to have been sealed off because its water content was as high as 99.8 per cent. But then it had dropped to 45 per cent, and the laboratory technician had asked her to get another sample to be quite sure. With the tin in her hand Xiao Tai hurried along the winding path. Her black eyes, set rather wide apart, showed no trace of fatigue, for she was sure she would receive a letter from Shi Jun that morning. The thought of him, a young man with a crewcut, a cynical mouth and cold eyes, made her slow down. When in his greasy overalls and boots he looked taller than in his baggy army trousers. He appeared rather lazy and sloppy, rather proud, taciturn and sarcastic. Xiao Tai had thought she had known him fairly well. But recently Shi Jun had accompanied his father south for medical treatment.

From the south Shi Jun had written Xiao Tai two letters, causing her comrades to make fun of her. Whatever for? They were the most commonplace letters which everybody could read. She stamped her feet in exasperation when teased. Yang Meng, an understanding girl, took one letter and read it aloud. That shut them up. Still someone asked mischievously, "Why didn't he write to me?"

A good question! Why did he write to her? Xiao Tai halted. On the horizon the huge sun was rising, its horizontal rays casting a rosy tint over the grassland, the path and the entire autumn scene. Collecting her thoughts, she hurried on. The fresh morning air and the sunlight filled her heart with a disturbing happiness, as if life were opening its beautiful arms to everyone.

Instead of taking the sample to the laboratory, she went to her room first. Yang Meng, small and thin, sat at the window as usual, reading a book on geology.

"Any letters?" Xiao Tai asked.

"Yes." She produced a letter from her folder and handed it to her. "From Shi Jun," she added.

Xiao Tai blushed at the mention of his name and said lamely, "I was wondering whether you'd received the admission notice from the university."

"No," Yang Meng replied in a low voice. But Xiao Tai was already too engrossed in her letter to hear her. Yang Meng went back to her reading.

Shi Jun had scribbled a sheet and a half in big characters. The other half was taken up by his signature. Another letter like the other two — one anybody could read, telling her that his father was being reinstated in his former post as Party secretary of a bureau and they would soon be returning to move house. But the last two lines made Xiao Tai's heart beat fast. "Hope to see you again. Tell me, please, how shall I introduce you to my father?"

What did he mean by that? She mulled that question over. Was this what she had been waiting for? Was it love? Then, conscious of Yang Meng's eyes on her, she said casually, "Shi Jun is coming back to move. His father is resuming his former post."

"Ah!" For some reason this news had made Yang Meng jump to her feet. Then, calming down, she picked up Xiao Tai's tin and told her, "I'll take this to the lab. You go to bed now."

Xiao Tai inquired again, "Any news from the university?"

Yang Meng shook her head and went away with the tin, her book and pen, her slight, spare figure like a flower that had withered before its time. Xiao Tai knew that some youngsters in other teams had received their admission notices already, but to mention this to her would have been cruel. When working in the countryside after she had left school, Yang Meng had been recommended three times by the peasants to go to university. Each time she lost her chance as the children of those with pull went in her place. Now that admission was by examination, she was a little over age. But Yang Meng never talked about her disappointments or seemed to have any burden on her mind. She spent all her time studying the neozoic, mesozoic and paleozoic strata formed hundreds of millions of years ago. At midnight, she would get up and go to the reading-room next door, pull down the lamp and immerse herself in what interested her most. Xiao Tai respected her but had never felt sorry for her. Now that she herself had this secret happiness, she suddenly pitied Yang Meng. Running after her she said consolingly, "Don't worry, Yang Meng. Things are different now from the times of the 'gang of four'. You did so well in the exams, they're bound to take you. I bet you'll receive the notice tomorrow."

Yang Meng smiled and nodded appreciatively by way of answer. Then she turned away, looking worn out and listless. Was Xiao Tai extra sensitive today, or was Yang Meng really tired? Slowly Xiao Tai washed her face and looked into the mirror at a paler than usual image of herself. Her eyes preoccupied, she dimpled as if asking, "How shall I introduce you?"

The eyes in the mirror dilated and darkened and her expression grew grave as she shook her head. "No, it's not that thing called love. Love is more beautiful. He didn't mean anything special. How to introduce me, indeed! Well, my name is Xiao Tai, that's all."

She quickly undressed and went to bed, ashamed of the fancies in which she had been indulging. Making her mind a blank she closed her eyes. Although it was autumn she found her thin quilt too warm. She kicked it loose and put her arms out. Reaching under her pillow, her fingers touched Shi Jun's letter, which she pulled out and re-read. "No, he must have meant something by this question. Only he's too proud to show his feelings and wants me to take the initiative. So this is love after all?" She closed her eyes again and let her thoughts wander as she relived their encounters over the years. . . .

One night in the autumn of 1975, Xiao Tai and many other young people who had been working in the countryside arrived at the oilfield by train. Over twenty of them, who had been assigned to oil-producing teams, waited at the headquarters for their teams to pick them up. Xiao Tai and a young man called Shi Jun were assigned to Team 303. Excited at the thought of her new post and wondering who her new work-mate was, Xiao Tai looked at the young men around her. Her eyes first rested on a bespectacled youth who seemed like a southerner; but he went off in the first truck. Next she decided it must be that ruddy faced northerner who was chatting away happily. But he soon went away with another team. In the end she was left with a bewhiskered cadre wearing no socks but a pair of old gym shoes. There was no Shi Jun.

Team 303 was the farthest away. At last their truck arrived. The girl who had come to welcome her was small and sallow. Her low forehead was lined and her age was hard to tell. Only her eyes were lively with youth. She shook Xiao Tai's hand with a powerful grip and introduced herself briefly with a slight Guangdong accent. "My name is Yang Meng. I arrived here two months ago."

"Did you go to the countryside after school too?" Xiao Tai was glad to have someone to talk to.

"Yes." She hoisted Xiao Tai's heavy luggage on to her shoulder effortlessly. Xiao Tai, stumbling behind her with a holdall, saw Yang Meng with one shrug of her shoulder tip the luggage neatly into the back of the truck, just as if she were a porter.

"How long were you in the countryside?" Xiao Tai asked.

"Eight years."

"What, eight years!" She was surprised. "You must be quite a bit older than me."

"Yes. I'm quite old." Yang Meng turned to smile at her for the first time. Seeing Xiao Tai's big eyes opened wide in astonishment, she asked as she lifted the holdall into the truck, "Are you twenty?"

Xiao Tai smiled wryly, showing two rows of fine white teeth. Her left cheek dimpled and her face lit up. "I'm twenty-one. And I've been independent and seen a lot of life for three years already which makes me look older than my age."

Giving her a friendly pat, Yang Meng told her, "Let's get on the truck, another comrade is waiting for us in town."

"You mean Shi Jun?" asked Xiao Tai as she clambered in.

"Right." Yang Meng climbed up the truck. Then the driver set off.

The truck had a canvas top and two rows of seats. Yang Meng sat near the front while Xiao Tai stood behind the cabin in the cold autumn wind, not wanting to miss the night scene. "I think the father of this Shi Jun must be a VIP," she remarked.

"He was."

"Then Shi Jun's all right. His father's former boss and comrades-in-arms will look after him. Do you know him?"

"No."

Hearing this Xiao Tai went on more boldly, "According to my experience, you either avoid these people who have important connections or play up to them."

Yang Meng smiled slightly. In the darkness Xiao Tai couldn't see her; besides, she was too engrossed in looking around, but she noticed that Yang Meng paused before answering softly, "They may have had important connections before. But now, they are much worse off than other people."

"Maybe. They find things hard which are nothing to the common run of people like us: settling down in the countryside, working in the fields, cooking, washing clothes and eating corn buns."

"You're right, but you've left out the burden on their minds."

"Maybe." Leaning over the truck and looking at the clusters of lights far and near, Xiao Tai couldn't help exclaiming, "What a beautiful sight!" Turning around she said, "I like dreaming. People say I'm sentimental, but I don't agree. I think I've learned something about the world these years. As you are older I hope you'll keep an eye on me from now on and advise me from time to time. I can see that you are a good honest person, staying in the countryside for eight whole years before being transferred. You can't have had any pull ...." As the truck stopped a small bedding-roll and a string-bag were thrown in and a young man heaved himself in. He was of medium height, with broad shoulders and a crew-cut. He ignored the two girls and sat down at the back, but they both knew he must be Shi Jun.

His presence chilled the atmosphere. It was some time before Xiao Tai broke the silence to ask, "You live in this town?"

He grunted by way of answer.

"Is this your hometown?"

"No."

"Then how come you live here?" she persisted.

"We were sent here." He spoke caustically, implying, "That should satisfy you!" Embarrassed, Xiao Tai fell silent and was thankful for the darkness. After a while a calm voice said, "I came here because fortune smiled upon me." It was Yang Meng. Xiao Tai dimpled. Still looking out she started to hum *Song of the Oil Workers*, but stopped when no one joined in. So the truck jolted along through the grassland carrying the three young people, all equally silent but entirely different in character.

Shi Jun and Xiao Tai hadn't seen each other very distinctly that night and the few sentences they exchanged were not friendly. The following day they met again, and Xiao Tai was most embarrassed by this encounter.

In the morning she went with Yang Meng to see an exhausted well with a water content of 99.8 per cent. When they came out of the team office the bare grassland lay before her vast and desolate. The mystery and beauty created by the lights on the derricks the previous night had vanished without a trace as if by magic. Leaning against a basketball rack, Xiao Tai's eyes brimmed over. Yang Meng glanced at her but made no effort to comfort her, simply standing beside her in silence. After a while Xiao Tai wiped away her tears.

"I'm a weakling, aren't I?" she said.

"You're too sentimental, but not necessarily weak. Don't you agree with me?"

"Yes, I do. That's what I think. And I'll show you by my actions that I'm not a weakling," she announced as tears streamed down her cheeks again. And it was just then that Shi Jun walked over to accost her.

"Are you Xiao Tai?"

She raised her tearful face. "Yes, I am."

As Shi Jun eyed her intently, the cynical twist of his lips disappeared. "You don't like it here?" he asked sincerely.

"No. And I've admitted it, unlike some others." Wiping away her tears she looked him challengingly in the face.

Glancing away he said, "Let's go and get our things, the three things oil workers can't do without — canteen, flashlight and a greatcoat."

He made no attempt to hide his own dejection. Xiao Tai was at a loss. The huge red sun sailed over the horizon and a flock of wild-geese flew south in a V formation. The three young people gazed after them until they disappeared. Looking at each other again they found they were standing in a V formation too.

Yang Meng broke the silence. "Our work is underground." Taking Xiao Tai by the hand she looked at Shi Jun and said, "The oil which has stayed underground for hundreds of millions of years will escape and go into hiding when pressure is put on it. We can spend a life-time studying it. Come on now, let's go to have a look at Well 48." With Yang Meng in the lead, the three young oil workers walked in a V formation along the path through the grassland.

"How shall I introduce you to my father?" Lying wide-eyed on the bed Xiao Tai turned this question over in her mind. Then the sound of soft sobbing made her sit up straight. It was stifled sobbing coming from the reading-room. Who was it? Yang Meng? No. Yang Meng would never sob like that. When she listened carefully again, the sound had stopped and all was silence. She lay down and heaved a deep sigh. "How shall I introduce you to my father?"

When had that question begun to arise? It was the first Spring Festival after Xiao Tai's arrival at the oil-field when the meandering path was still covered with snow. Xiao Tai and those who had been on home leave had all returned, but Shi Jun whose home was in town was two weeks overdue. He had gone to the provincial city to visit relatives. The team leader was furious and had criticized him in meetings big and small. One afternoon, during a meeting, Shi Jun hurried in panting and sweating. He was wearing a worn-out red sweat shirt and had a padded jacket under one arm. As soon as he sat down the team leader bellowed, "Stand up, Shi Jun."

Everyone present was taken aback. Shi Jun, surprised at first, sat back more comfortably in the chair and demanded, "What is it?"

"Stand up and tell us why you are late." The team leader was still more incensed by his attitude.

"Can't you hear me if I'm seated?" Shi Jun looked squarely at the team leader. Xiao Tai clenched her sweaty hands, disapproving of the way the team leader had stormed at Shi Jun before finding out why he was late.

"You.... Get out of here!" The enraged team leader dashed over meaning to throw him out. Shi Jun remained seated while he wiped the sweat from his chin on one shoulder, then silently he took his padded coat and made for the door. Xiao Tai felt a deep sympathy for him, and regretted now what she had said about him that first evening before they met.

After the meeting she went to seek out Shi Jun who was standing alone in the playground, leaning against the basketball rack deep in thought. Before she got there someone took her arm. It was Yang Meng who said to her softly, "The hardest thing for a person to bear is not a dressing-down or beating, but loneliness, ostracism."

They walked up to Shi Jun. Yang Meng smiled at him while Xiao Tai fumed, "Take no notice of a fellow like that."

"I'm used to him. What can he do but make things difficult for someone like me?" Shi Jun leaned despondently against the rack.

"It's not their fault. They have to behave that way to protect themselves," said Yang Meng, her eyes on the golden setting sun above the horizon.

"Yes. It doesn't matter if they crack down on us. They have their official posts to think about," Xiao Tai put in. Then she asked Shi Jun, "Where have you been all this time?"

"I went to the prison. Maybe you didn't know that my father has been imprisoned as a secret agent." He watched Xiao Tai's face intently with cold penetrating eyes.

She was at a loss for words.

"How is Comrade Shi Yifeng?" inquired Yang Meng. This time Shi Jun fell silent. After some time he replied, "Fine, thank you. You know my father?"

"No, I've heard about him." The setting sun turned crimson.

"You went with your mother?" Xiao Tai asked more gently.

Shi Jun shook his head, "My mother was a brave weakling. The year after my father's imprisonment, that is, the year after our family was sent here, she took a whole bottle of sleeping-pills and never woke up."

Xiao Tai gave an exclamation of dismay, but Yang Meng's face was expressionless, only her long eyelashes quivered as she lowered them to cover her burning eyes. After a while she touched Shi Jun softly on the shoulder and asked in a steady voice, "But didn't you tell us you went home every weekend to see your mother?"

"To see her ashes and my younger sister whom she left in my care. She's thirteen and studying. Children hold their lives cheap, so I have to go home to give her some warmth and faith. I want her to have faith in our father, to believe that he isn't a criminal. Mother died because she had lost faith. My sister can go hungry but she mustn't lose her courage and faith in life."

Yang Meng thought for some time and then said, "To believe in your father's innocence isn't enough. You must teach her as well as yourself not to waste your time while you're waiting, not to be soft with yourselves but to work and study hard. She's lucky to be able to go to school and to have a brother to look after her." She left abruptly leaving Xiao Tai behind.

Her eyes filled with tears, Xiao Tai asked him, "Is there anything I can do?" Slowly, Shi Jun shook his head.

The evening rays had lost their colour. A few thin clouds hung in the sky. In the twilight everything seemed pure and calm.

The sobbing was heard again. This time, even softer,

it was more nerve-racking. Xiao Tai tossed and turned in her bed. Then she sat up, but decided not to get dressed and go out to satisfy her curiosity. So she lay down again but couldn't go to sleep, though she was very tired. Gradually the sobbing stopped and silence returned. But Xiao Tai still lay in bed with wide-opened eyes.

The following Sunday, Yang Meng woke Xiao Tai up very early. When she had got up and washed her hair, Yang Meng suggested, "I've a mind to visit Shi Jun and see what I can do for him. Would you like to go too?"

"Yes, certainly. It's a marvellous idea. Why didn't it occur to me?" Xiao Tai jumped with joy. Yang Meng rubbed her soft dark hair dry, and then, putting her hands on Xiao Tai's shoulders, she told her, "The idea is good, but it just happens that I'm busy today. Can you go alone?"

"Certainly." Xiao Tai nodded in bewilderment.

Very pleased, Yang Meng pressed her nose playfully and told her, "You are like the beautiful kind-hearted girl called Snow White I read about when I was small. Now make haste and go. If any clothes need mending you can bring them back to me."

As the short northern spring had started, the wind was less biting. The path twisted through the yellow grassland. Along it drifted what seemed like a mauve flower, a flower with rosy cheeks and a flickering smile set off by a woollen scarf. How would Shi Jun receive her, Xiao Tai wondered.

Shi Jun's home was at the edge of the small town. At the gate there were two stone steps leading into a long courtyard which had at one end a well, at the other a well-tended lilac. When Xiao Tai walked in, Shi Jun was kneading dough. He was not surprised to see her, but came over to ask, "What is it?"

"Nothing," said the embarrassed girl. "I've come to see your sister."

"Oh!" More at ease, he said, "She's not in. She has gone to visit a classmate." Still standing at the door, he had shown no inclination to invite her in. Xiao Tai was disappointed at not receiving the warm and excited welcome she had expected. But now, she had to stand at the door awkwardly and tell him frankly, "I've come to see if there's anything I can do." She pushed him aside to enter the room which was partitioned into two by a sheet hanging in the middle. Virtually bare except for two wooden beds, the room was nevertheless in a state of disorder. Shi Jun followed her with a glum face. It was hard to tell whether he was pleased or annoyed.

"He's too proud." She pretended not to have noticed anything and unpicked the quilts, putting the covers in a basin beside the well. The sheets were too old to stand much scrubbing. "Yang Meng was right," she sighed. "Now they're much worse off than other people." Then she collected a large bundle of clothes and socks to be mended. Shi Jun watched her, neither preventing, helping, nor thanking her. When Xiao Tai was ready to go, he blocked the door with one arm on the frame. Fixing cold eyes on her he demanded, "Is this sympathy or pity?"

Xiao Tai had felt sorry for him. Now pity welled up in her. His pride was wounded. So she told him sincerely, "Aren't we colleagues and comrades, Shi Jun?"

"So you have come to do some good deeds." His mouth twisted cynically again.

"What's wrong with that?"

"I don't need it. I have no use for kindness and charity, don't you understand?" He was so agitated that the veins on his forehead throbbed. He seemed to be challenging Xiao Tai to a fight.

But she smiled and replied, "I understand." She preferred this to gratitude. Though too worked up, he had won her respect. Smiling she told him, "Suppose I have this urge to do something? I have time. And I'm interested in doing these things. Now, aren't you satisfied?" Pushing him aside as she had when she came in, she left.

"You're lying." Shi Jun caught up with her.

"I never lie." She stopped abruptly. She had not told the truth. Turning around, her big eyes on him, she said gravely, "The truth is, it was Yang Meng's idea — I just carried it out."

Shi Jun nodded, his eyes burning as he looked back and said, "Since you have this urge, I hope you'll come again next Sunday, but on your own initiative please."

Xiao Tai had to avoid his eyes. Turning away she said, "What a lovely lilac."

"We brought it with us from the south."

"I see."

This was her first visit and Xiao Tai felt happier on her way home. Was it because she had done a good deed, or for some other reason? She couldn't tell. All she knew was that she was happy, and the grassland seemed less desolate and yellow. She returned to her quarters like a successful adventurer. In the evening Yang Meng and she looked over the bundle of clothes.

Smoothing them out, Yang Meng sighed. "His life was better than average in the past. So now when he lives the same hard life as others, it's harder for him."

"You seem to know him well, Yang Meng, and to feel for him deeply."

She hesitated before answering, "Possibly."

"But he has no use for sympathy."

"In that case he shouldn't give people reason to sympathize."

Yang Meng, a thimble on one finger, quickly and neatly mended a sleeve while Xiao Tai was still clumsily darning a sock.

Though Yang Meng helped with the mending, and though Xiao Tai and Shi Jun had no more contact than usual, word spread that they had fallen in love. Both denied the rumour, Shi Jun with a long face saying, "Don't make fun of me. I have no place for love," while Xiao Tai giggled and holding up some mended clothes declared, "Pity. These were mended by Yang Meng."

Xiao Tai didn't go to Shi Jun's home again the following Sunday as he had hoped. She went three weeks later to return the clothes. This time she found Shi Jun's home cleaner, and the fire burning merrily. Shi Jun, wearing a sweat shirt, was writing a letter. He was pleased to see Xiao Tai, and greeted her jestingly with, "Ah, the angel has come."

But Xiao Tai had not answered in the way Yang Meng had wished. She announced, "Most of these were mended by Yang Meng. So I'm not the angel." Scanning the room she asked, "Where's your sister? Gone to see a classmate again?"

"No, one of my father's fellow officers in the army came to take her away, telling me that he knew my father well and didn't believe he was a secret agent." Shi Jun laughed. It was the first time Xiao Tai had seen him laugh.

"It seems that he is the real angel of your family," said she, regretting that the clothes Yang Meng and she had sat up late to mend would not be needed by his sister any more.

"I don't believe in angels." His smile vanishing, a coldness returned to his eyes. "These last few years I have come to believe in 'conditions'. Conditions and interests determine everything. The attitude towards us of some relatives and friends changed completely when my father got into trouble. Others weren't so open about it but they put on airs, as if condescending to us. I preferred the former to the latter. This new development may be a sign that my father will be cleared pretty soon."

His words, frank and truthful, made a shiver run down Xiao Tai's back. Looking at Shi Jun and then at the pile of clothes she had brought back she said, "I hope you won't look upon this as a sign of charity. This is friendship. If you think friendship imposes conditions too, pay me twenty cents for what I've done."

"You got me wrong." He lowered his eyes and said reluctantly, "I told you that just because I believe in your disinterested friendship."

"Then you admit that in our society there exist things of value and of beauty."

"Yes. What you did made me realize that."

"Not just me. Mainly Yang Meng."

"I know," Shi Jun said impatiently, "I noticed you announced that last time. You seem to have a great respect for her. Do you know her well?"

"She hardly ever talks about herself. She's sincere and studies hard. She's concerned about you too."

"I think this scholar should be more concerned about herself. I see that most of her letters come from a farm — a labour reform camp."

"Is that so!" Now things made more sense to Xiao Tai. "That's why she understands your needs and predicament so well and has such concern for you. She must have had a similar experience."

"Not necessarily," Shi Jun said stiffly, as if insulted.

Xiao Tai remembered Yang Meng, old before her time, poring over a book at midnight under a lamp pulled down to her head, and the motherly way she mended with a thimble on her finger. She had remained optimistic and confident while befriending others unobtrusively.

"You're right," she nodded. "You're different."

"But I'm grateful to her for sending you here," said Shi Jun, eyeing her searchingly.

In some confusion Xiao Tai swung round to look out of the window at the lilac just turning green.

"That's a good lilac," she remarked at random.

"You've said that before," Shi Jun smiled. Xiao Tai's cheeks turned scarlet. He added softly, "We brought it here from the south and we'll take it back with us."

"I'm sure you will." Feeling that he was putting pressure on her which made her uncomfortable she rose to leave.

Shi Jun saw her to the door, saying, "Though my sister's gone I hope you'll go on showing concern for me, will you?"

Xiao Tai thought for a while before she answered, "Do you need it?"

"Sure." He gripped her hands.

Xiao Tai blushed again. Pulling her hands away she fled. Oppressed by the consciousness of a pair of eyes gazing after her, she quickened her steps.

Since then she had returned only once with many comrades in October 1976. Then, this summer, Shi Jun's father had been cleared of the false charges against him. Shi Jun was overjoyed when the authorities told him to take his father down south to convalesce. When he came to say goodbye to Xiao Tai he had taken the liberty of putting his arm around her waist and shouting, "We've won. Hurrah!" He then hurried off along that meandering path before Xiao Tai could figure out whether this was an expression of love or he had just forgotten himself in his jubilation.

Then he had sent her those two commonplace letters and now this one with the question, "How shall I introduce you to my father?" Xiao Tai sat up abruptly. She must seek out Yang Meng and talk to her. Just as she was putting on her clothes, Yang Meng came softly in. In her hand was a thick letter in a big envelope. Surprised to find Xiao Tai awake, she quickly stuck the envelope under her pillow and came over to sit on her bed. "Can't you sleep?" she asked, forcing a smile.

Xiao Tai shook her head, then taking her hand she inquired, "You've been crying, Yang Meng. Has the university turned you down?"

"Yes. But I was prepared for that. I'm over age. Now that they're starting to recruit research students again, next year I'll sit for that. Well 48 is back in production. Though the percentage of water is high it proves that some of my theories regarding geological analysis are correct. Once this well is back to normal I shall have a good sound basis for my theories. Then I'll write a paper. You won't laugh at me, will you?" Yang Meng's eyes shone with excitement.

Xiao Tai was overwhelmed with admiration for the steadfast girl in front of her whose eyes were still swollen from crying. She said solemnly, "I'm sure you can do anything you've set your heart on, Yang Meng."

"No. I'll have to study English very hard for a year. Now let me tell you some good news. Shi Jun has come back with his father. He just phoned our team leader telling him that they are leaving very soon. He wants you to go to see him. Shall I congratulate you, Xiao Tai?"

Xiao Tai's reaction was unexpected. She looked at Yang Meng solemnly and asked, "Tell me what love is. Have you ever experienced it?"

Yang Meng fell silent. After a while she replied, "I've never experienced love, Xiao Tai. I've only had a proposal of marriage."

This time Xiao Tai was silent. Staring at Yang Meng unseeingly, she kept asking herself, "Is this love? Should we get married? Do I love him? And what do I see in him?"

Yang Meng's voice came to her as if from far far away, "Shi Jun is leaving too, of course. The team leader said that he's going back to the province where his father's posted and may go to an oil research institute or geological institute."

"What's all that got to do with me?" mumbled Xiao Tai.

"Maybe nothing. Maybe a great deal. When will you go to see him?"

"I don't know. I might go this evening," Xiao Tai heard herself replying. Dazed she saw Yang Meng take out the big envelope and hurry off, telling her that she had something to attend to. Left by herself the question recurred to her, "How shall I introduce you to my father?"

"Let's bring this to a head and get it over with." Xiao Tai got up and, not stopping to change her clothes, set off to town. The track twisted so much that she tried to take a short cut, but she soon returned to the path, which was easier to walk on. On she trudged, her hands in her pockets, feeling emotionally enervated by the grassland's desolation, or was it that Yang Meng's strength had shown up her weakness? Anyway, she felt melancholy. Countless times she had dreamed of, longed for and waited for love. It should be as mysterious and beautiful as the moon in the water or flowers in a light mist, pure, sparkling and passionate, playing on one's heart-strings. Yet in reality at close hand it was entirely different. Xiao Tai was bewildered, not knowing which was correct — real life or her imagination.

"Everything is conditional," Shi Jun had said and he might be right.

It was late afternoon when the two stone steps came into view. Her heart beating fast, she regretted having come so early; things would have been more convenient by moonlight or lamplight. She was hesitating when she saw Yang Meng walk down the steps and hurry away. This unexpected encounter made Xiao Tai walk straight over and in. It was an entirely different room now with the luggage and chests all packed. Shi Jun was putting some things into a small suitcase.

"Was Yang Meng here?" Xiao Tai asked eagerly.

Shi Jun turned around. He had put on weight. Smiling at her he said, "I knew you would come."

Xiao Tai had to ask again, "Has Yang Meng been here?"

"Oh, yes, she came to see my father, but he had gone to a farewell dinner. I stayed behind to wait for you." He moved the suitcase off the stool so that she could sit down.

Xiao Tai saw a thick letter on the table addressed to Comrade Shi Yifeng. "Then she didn't see him?" she asked.

"Who?"

"Yang Meng didn't see your father?"

"No. It was useless anyway." Shi Jun threw up his hands in a helpless way and laughed wryly. "You see, even before my father has taken up his post people ask him for favours. Yang Meng's father worked under my father in the past. He got into trouble in 1957 and is now still working on a farm." A soft, stifled sobbing sounded in Xiao Tai's ears. As it was very hot, Shi Jun unbuttoned his shirt at the neck and sat down on a chest. "She wrote a letter saying that her father had been wronged and that he was now over sixty, and inquiring if his former unit could arrange for him to leave the farm. I can understand how she feels, but
. . . ."

"But what?"

"Nothing. How can my father attend to this sort of thing as soon as he resumes office? Besides, the one who wronged her father is still in power."

Xiao Tai sat there woodenly, staring at a pile of waste paper and discarded clothes and socks which Yang Meng and she had mended. Their uselessness justified throwing them away. Still she couldn't help feeling sad. After a while she stood up to take her leave. "Your father will be late. I won't wait for him. When do you leave? I'll come to see you off."

"Three twenty tomorrow afternoon," he replied mechanically, looking perplexed, not having expected such a fleeting visit. He stood up in a flurry and only strode over when Xiao Tai was almost at the door. As his throat was too constricted to utter her name, he blocked the door with one arm as he had done at her first visit while his other hand remained in his trouser pocket. His head half turned, his teeth clenched, he still couldn't get a word out. They stood close to each other in silence. Xiao Tai was surprised to find herself so calm, even her early nervousness had gone. The little courtyard was different too, with the leafy lilac lying on the ground, its roots carefully wrapped up.

"Taking it south?" she asked quietly.

"Yes. I told you that it would be going back south, remember?" His confidence and calm returning, he asked, "Will you go back too, Xiao Tai? Have you given my question any thought?"

"You mean how to introduce me to your father? My name is Xiao Tai, your colleague and comrade, and I'm from the south too," she said playfully.

"You think that's all? This is no joke, Xiao Tai. It concerns your future."

"Maybe it does." Her voice surprised her. She was talking as calmly as in a small group meeting. "But one should work hard for one's future, shouldn't one?" She seemed to see Yang Meng's bright eyes looking at her.

Shi Jun gazed at her for a long time before saying, "You came to see and help me when I was in trouble. That's something I treasure."

Xiao Tai was touched, yet at a loss. "Shi Jun," she said. "You want to know the truth? I don't know what to think. Sympathy, the chance of a better job and a better life — these are not love. But sometimes they seem very like it, being closely bound up together. I, well, I just don't know."

"You silly girl," he exclaimed, grasping her hands. "I didn't expect this of you. Think it over before giving me an answer. I'll be waiting."

Xiao Tai nodded and pulled away her hands saying, "I'll come to see you off tomorrow." With that she left.

The sun was setting, its afterglow giving a splendid serenity to the grassland and the path running across it. On this narrow track Xiao Tai walked slowly. A voice seemed to be saying in her heart, "How lovely to return to the south like that lilac!" This was something of which she and her mother had dreamed. It could come true if she accepted Shi Jun. That was probably what her mother had meant when she said that a girl was born twice into the world. Where did love come in then? Was she going to marry the south, a better job and, perhaps, better meals too? Love needed a full stomach, but the two were quite different things. That inner voice said again, "Don't pretend you have no feeling for Shi Jun. It may not be very deep, but it can develop. Why make it sound so bad by talking about marrying the south? Why be so strict with yourself? Shi Jun hasn't gone yet. It's not too late."

Only the small path witnessed the girl's passionate preoccupation as she walked along pondering the true meaning of friendship and love. And her wayward thoughts had their parallel in the twists and turns of the path.

Back at the team Xiao Tai wanted to console Yang Meng and confide in her all her contradictions and her decision. But Yang Meng was not in the room. At the window where she used to sit was a canvas holdall. "Has she been admitted to the university?" she wondered. But she found out from other people that Yang Meng had received a telegram saying that her father was seriously ill; she had been granted leave and gone to buy a train ticket.

Xiao Tai flopped down on her bed, totally exhausted, without even the energy to take off her shoes. She remembered that she had skipped supper but she didn't feel like eating. She just lay there as darkness closed in. Later it would make way for light again. This was like the cycle of the seasons in which life went on with each one carrying his or her own burdens, each with personal hopes and ideals, joys and sorrows. Life was pressing past Xiao Tai like flowing water, impelling her along. The easiest way was to drift with the current and let matters take their own course. Otherwise one must fight hard, especially in the beginning. But Xiao Tai was tired and presently she dozed off.

At midnight she was woken by Yang Meng. She clutched her friend's hands and sat up. "Is there anything I can do for you?" she asked. "You mustn't worry too much." But she realized that comfort was unnecessary when she saw Yang Meng's greasy overalls, hair wet with sweat and face flushed with excitement.

Keeping her voice down but unable to hide her elation Yang Meng told her, "Xiao Tai, our plan will soon succeed. Well 48 can be revived. Do you hear me, Xiao Tai?" Taking off her wet overalls she wiped her hair with them and, laughing happily, tousled Xiao Tai's hair saying, "Just think of it, Xiao Tai. Well 48 resurrected! Even if it produces only fifty tons of oil a day, that means five thousand dollars. And the paper I've planned to write. But I'm going away tomorrow. I'll be back within a fortnight. In the meantime you must carry on with our experiments." She handed her a folder.

Xiao Tai sat woodenly on the bed. Yang Meng was like a fresh breeze clearing her mind. She had never seen her so happy or voluble before. She had been swimming in the current of life inconspicuous and unnoticed, swimming slowly and steadily towards the goal she had set herself. Her determination far surpassed the encouragement Xiao Tai had prepared to give her. Taking over the folder Xiao Tai nodded, unable to utter a word. When she had dried her hair, Yang Meng sat down beside her.

"A penny for your thoughts, Xiao Tai," she said.

"I'm a weakling after all."

"To realize one's weakness is a sign of strength, don't you agree?" After pausing she continued, "In mechanics, an external agent puts something still into action. It's like a bridge leading you to the other side. But in real life, this bridge is sometimes frighteningly narrow, or sometimes as beautiful as a rainbow. It's entirely up to you to choose where you want to go after crossing this bridge. You understand me?"

Xiao Tai clutched Yang Meng's hand and nodded. This was a parting gift from Yang Meng as well as the declaration of her belief.

"Fine. It's time to go to your shift now."

Xiao Tai had almost forgotten that her shift was starting. She quickly threw a padded jacket over her shoulders, took a flashlight and hurried out. But she ran back to ask, "What time does your train leave, Yang Meng?"

"Tomorrow, no, this afternoon at three twenty."

Yang Meng had already left for the station when Xiao Tai returned from work. She had a meal, slept for a while, then changed her clothes and went to Shi Jun's home. As she mounted the two stone steps, she had a feeling that she had come too late. The room was empty except for the furniture borrowed from the oil-field. A sense of loss brought on a tender longing. "Go to the station and tell him we are closer than colleagues and comrades. . . ." As she turned in a flurry to leave, she caught sight of a pile of neatly folded clothes on which was a note which read:

Xiao Tai,

We are leaving early for the station to check in our luggage. Please return these overalls for me. Hoping to see you at the station,

Shi Jun

She tenderly picked up the clothes. Then a big envelope among a pile of waste-paper attracted her attention. "That's Yang Meng's letter. They've forgotten to take it along." She picked it up, intending to take it to the station. But the letter was torn into two. She sat down on the bed. They hadn't forgotten it, only forgotten to throw it away somewhere else. Xiao Tai couldn't help putting the letter together on the table to read the lines Yang Meng had written in tears.

Comrade Shi Yifeng,

You may remember a man called Yang Shichang who worked under you in 1957 when you were the secretary of the bureau Party committee. You know how he was punished and sent to a farm for labour reform just because he had written a letter making some suggestions and some criticisms of the bureau's work. I was only eight at the time. And because of that I was not able to be a Young Pioneer and wear a red scarf. But I sent my father the good marks I got at school to encourage him to remould himself. Two years later when he was no longer looked upon as a criminal we were overjoyed. But then we learned that once somebody had committed a "mistake" he was a marked man for life. He had to go on working on this farm. Seeing no future, my mother committed suicide just as Shi Jun's mother did. Only twelve years old I was left with a brother of eight. . . .

Xiao Tai's hands were cold and she was shivering. Her watch read half past two and the station was some distance away, but she had no strength to stand up. Wiping away her tears she read on.

Now that your family have also suffered under the "gang of four's" false charges I believe you can understand my anguish and difficulties at that time. Our Party is now restoring the fine tradition of seeking truth from the facts and today, when everybody is rejoicing, may I also request. . . ?

As Xiao Tai rose slowly, her watch showed a quarter to three. She must go to the station, to see Yang Meng off and Shi Jun too. She folded up the torn letter, picked up the overalls and abruptly left the room and its narrow courtyard.

The bell had already rung by the time Xiao Tai reached the station, and people who were seeing off their friends began getting off the train. A group of cadres gathered at the door of the soft-sleeper carriage. Shi Jun leaning half out was shaking their hands while his eyes searched around. When he saw Xiao Tai he cried, "Write to me, Xiao Tai. I'll be waiting." Then the head of a greying man appeared beside him, thin, clean and healthy. This must be Shi Jun's father. Apparently Shi Jun was telling him about Xiao Tai, for he nodded kindly and waved to her. The train lurched forward.

In the next hard-seat carriage Yang Meng sat meditatively at the window. At sight of Xiao Tai, she immediately put her rough hand on the window-pane. Tears filling her eyes, Xiao Tai waved her handkerchief vigorously as the train gathered speed.

The people dispersed and Xiao Tai walked slowly away. Then she quickened her pace, wanting to go out to the grassland into the breeze. She wanted to walk on that twisting path, to ponder what course to take through the swirling stream of life.

Translated by Yu Fanqin

Huang Zongying in 1981

Huang Zongying

HUANG Zongying, born in Beijing in 1925, has had a chequered career. Her father, an engineer, died when she was nine, leaving the family impoverished. In 1946, she started acting in Shanghai and made her first film *Pursuit*. In '49, she married the great actor Zhao Dan. In '56, she joined the Party. In '58 she started writing articles and poems. The next year her first film script *The Common Cause* was filmed. In '63 she began writing reportage. During the ten years of turmoil her husband was arrested and she was persecuted.

Huang Zongying has travelled widely in China living with peasants as well as factory workers, and has visited the Soviet Union, Poland, Vietnam and America. In '78 she attended a natural science conference as a guest correspondent, and there met the heroine of "The Flight of the Wild-geese". She received national awards for this reportage and for "Beautiful Eyes". She is now a Special Science Policy Research Fellow of the State Scientific and Technological Commission.

The Flight of the Wild-Geese

Huang Zongying

Her

IN the spring of 1978, the trees and grass were turning green all over the land. I, who know nothing at all about science, found myself at the National Science Conference as a special correspondent.

I squeezed into the first bus taking correspondents to the Great Wall. There I climbed to a vantage point.

Scientists, advanced in years but fit, walked slowly up, while young girls, laughing and joking, challenged each other to a race. Catching sight of a girl standing against the wall gazing into the distance at the wild-geese flying north, I went up to her and asked, "A penny for your thoughts." Immediately I realized my mistake. As she turned around, I saw grey hairs at her temples and lines on her dark face. Calmly, she looked at me from behind her spectacles and gave me a slight smile. "The wild-geese remind me of the botanical gardens below the Wild-goose Pagoda in Xi'an," she explained.

"You're. . . ?"

"I grow wild medicinal herbs."

The racing girls, the herb grower and myself shared our picnic food and chatted about everything imaginable. Life is like that. Sometimes people can work together for years and still remain strangers. Sometimes they become friends as soon as they meet. The woman growing wild herbs aroused my interest for some unknown reason. Perhaps for her frankness, her composure, or perhaps because she looked as ordinary as any country midwife, who interrupts her pig-feeding and washes her hands before picking up her sterilized instruments. I sensed she was a scientist working among the peasants. I had been searching for someone to write about among the five thousand delegates. Perhaps she was my heroine. Since ordinary people are in the majority, I felt I should look among them for somebody to represent our generation of scientists.

Qin Guanshu, born in 1929, was an assistant research fellow at Xi'an Botanical Gardens in Shaanxi.

The following day, I and two other correspondents interviewed her.

Women scientists and writers are few in our country. As soon as we met, we were surrounded by cameras and tape recorders, making it difficult for us to talk. The flash bulbs lit up her grey hair. She looked older than her forty-nine years, yet there was something attractive about her. Her mouth and eyes showed her idealism. Her devotion to her work showed in her face.

That night after I had returned from a performance, I saw a neatly folded note on my desk. I opened it and read the beautiful handwriting:

> Dear Reporter,
> Thank you for your support and encouragement. But please don't write about me. I'm in a difficult position. I hope you will understand.
> Qin Guanshu

Her

She was not simply being modest. So what was it? I must get to the bottom of it.

I went to the Shaanxi delegation and asked for the notes on their delegates. I was handed a big pile. I spent an evening poring over them, but could not find the name of Qin Guanshu.

I returned the pile the following morning. "There's nothing about Qin Guanshu. Why? Can you help me find her notes?"

Two days later I was told apologetically that nothing about her had been sent to Beijing since she was not an advanced worker. The delegation had brought no information about her either. There was only a simple form filled in by Xi'an Botanical Gardens. Then I was recommended to follow up the other advanced women scientists from Shaanxi. Why was I interested in this unknown person?

From other sources, I found out that there had been differences of opinion about her attending the conference. She had not been nominated. Even now, she was not considered a proper delegate.

Why was she in such a difficult situation? I was even more interested in establishing the truth.

I enlisted the help of Yang Ge, vice-chairman of the Shaanxi delegation and vice-director of the Shaanxi Commission of Science and Technology, and Liu Kang, another vice-director of the commission.

I liked Liu Kang, a woman like myself. She expressed the hope that I would go to Shaanxi to investigate the matter. I asked the comrades of the Shaanxi delegation to contact Xi'an Botanical Gardens on my behalf so that I could go and write a small reportage on Qin.

I got the permission near the end of the conference.

Her??

It was months before I had time to go to Xi'an.

Xi'an is the pride of the Chinese nation, where many talented poets like Li Bai and Du Fu and great writers once lived. The Buddhist sutras brought back from India by the monk Xuanzang are housed in the Big Wild-goose Pagoda, beneath which stretch the botanical gardens. Why were the gardens, instead of being green, so desolate? Within its new walls how much research was being carried out? How many personnel had it trained? How many contributions had it made towards modernization? As the saying goes, "The field, the sleeves and the stove show how good the farmer, the seamstress and the cooks are." The weeds and leaves on the footpaths, the plants growing at random, regardless of species, the broken benches in the laboratories — what did these signify?

I was anxious and worried, not because of the sabotage done by the "gang of four", but because after their fall my hosts still had not done anything to improve their work. What were they waiting for?

I began to make investigations concerning Qin.

Some people I met were impressed by her helping the medicinal herb company in the mountains, which meant being absent from her family for long periods of time. Other opinions varied. Many were negative!

They said she kept aloof from people, that she was bad tempered, arrogant and quarrelsome.

They claimed she was too individualistic, hoping to gain fame and become an expert.

They pointed out she was the daughter of a landlord and had not broken with her reactionary family.

They described how she did not accept the criticisms people made of her during the "cultural revolution" with good grace.

They also said she had not wanted to go into the mountains and grow wild medicinal herbs. She only went because her superiors persuaded her to do so.

I was very disappointed. Why had I picked upon such a person to write about?

I went to see the Party secretary of the botanical gardens who told me like a politician, "Go ahead and write. It will encourage Qin to do a better job. I can explain to others. Although she has her faults, we must make allowances for her being a woman."

"Really?" I was shocked. Was that how her superiors looked at her? Being a woman myself, I objected to this. Since they had so much against her, why did they agree I should write about her? What approach should I take? What could I write?

Having come such a long way, I did not feel like packing up and going home. Had they sent the wrong delegate to Beijing or had I chosen the wrong person to write about? Yet why had her place of work, the medicinal herb company in Luonan County, strongly recommended her?

I had got involved in something beyond the scope of a reportage. So I went to see Liu Kang again and told her what I thought. After a pause she replied,

"Of course, I can't force you to write. But, since you're here, why not do some investigation? If the company was wrong to send her and we should not have given the consent, you can help us to find out the truth. We can learn a lesson from this. I can't believe you're the kind of person to give up an unsolved mystery without trying getting to the bottom of it. Why don't you make a trip to the Qinling Mountains? It's worth going. I'm all for writers visiting the scenic spots, if they're not extravagant. Seeing is better than hearing. Go. It's not important whether you write about her or not."

Her

I and some others went by car to the Qinling Mountains. On the plateau the wheat was harvested and the persimmons were bearing fruit.

En route, staff from the botanical gardens pointed out the trees to me: Lacquer trees, pristache, maples and dogwood. Pink roses nodded to us. Blackbirds splashed water from the river. Patches of purple and white grew on the ridges, slopes, levelled land and river banks. But what about Qin?

We got out at the Luonan Medicinal Herb Company. A power plant, formerly a temple, was supplying electricity to the little town. Qin was gathering in her laundry and a padded jacket. Mountain people knew that they needed heavy clothes in the mornings and evenings even in hot summer. The Shaanxi Party committee had telephoned her the night before. Qin had got up early and travelled 80 *li* back to the county town from a village on Heizhang Mountain, 2,000 metres above sea level. She had just finished giving lessons in a ballon-flower training class and had come to meet me.

Qin lived in a room beside the laboratory. I was given a room on the other side of it.

After supper, the little town was very quiet. Both of us were tired after our day's travel, and I was not eager to start talking seriously. Washing my feet, I sat on a stool in her room, refreshed by the hot water. As we chatted, I couldn't help saying in a roundabout way, "Now that you've attended the National Science Conference, your social status is different. You should mix in better with others...."

Slowly she folded her patched, homespun clothes, smoothing and pressing them.

Silently, she took out a packet of cigarettes and offered me one, throwing me a nonchalant glance. We two working women, who had learned to smoke during the "cultural revolution", were seldom bold enough to smoke in public. Now we sat facing each other watching the rising smoke. The silence oppressed me. I threw the water into the courtyard, saying to myself, "Let her sort out her own problems. I've done what I could."

"Well, well, Huang Zongying, we've been expecting you for years," Wang, the manager of the medicinal herb company, told me in his office, as he poured me a cup of tea.

I laughed. "I was told the people in the mountains are simple, but you've certainly got a sense of humour. I only decided to come a few months ago. How can you have been expecting me for years?"

"I'm telling the truth," he argued. "We've been

hoping that writers and reporters would come here to write about Qin. I can't write. I can only draw maps. Look. . . ." He turned on a fluorescent light. On one wall was a map of Luonan County. It was dotted with red like a big piece of red bean cake.

"Our county used to grow a lot of medicinal herbs in the past. On the mountains there were narrow-leaved polygala, wrinkled giant hyssop, ballon-flower, magnoliavine, red-rooted salvia, pinellia, honeysuckle and dendrobium. They decreased over the years. After Liberation, the government attached great importance to medicinal herbs so now, with the development of medicine and public hygiene, the demand for medicinal herbs cannot meet the needs. Since 1966, our county began to grow wild herbs on farms. We started with forty *mu* of land." He pointed at a few red dots. "We planned to reach 390 *mu* by 1970, but we reached only 226 *mu*." He pointed at a few more red dots. "In 1970, we asked Xi'an Botanical Gardens to send us some helpers. After Qin and a few others came, the situation changed. In 1977, 11,000 *mu* were planted by the county, the people's communes and the production brigades. Look. . . ." He swept his hand over the red dots. "In 1978, we cultivated 16,500 *mu*, 73 times as much as in 1970."

"Do you take over land allocated for crops?"

"Except for a few experimental plots, most of the herbs are grown on ridges, slopes and reclaimed land. How can we use good land to plant medicinal herbs when 90 per cent of our land here is mountains and rivers?"

"Can the herbs improve the soil and people's lives?"

"Yes. That's why we have a deep respect for Qin.

She worked hard to set up these farms. She's been to more mountains than we have, endured more hardships than us and solved problems we couldn't. She's won our respect. She has worked on all the farms and guides us with her scientific knowledge. Otherwise we wouldn't have dared to grow so much. Before she came, the more we planted the more money we lost. One winter, we lost 20,000 yuan on gastrodia alone. But now. . . ." Wang pointed at two charts on another wall, showing the development of medicinal herbs over the years, the quantity the county planned to purchase and the profit they had actually made.

The arrow rose higher every year. I joked, "This year, the arrow will pierce the roof!"

"The profit in 1970 was 320,400 yuan. It will reach a million this year, solving to some extent the lack of medicinal herbs in our country. From losing money the company now hands in more profit every year. Most of the brigades can now give free medical treatment to their members. As their income increases, they are able to mechanize agriculture. Vice-director Liu of the Shaanxi Commission of Science and Technology was pleased with our progress. . . ."

I interrupted, "Liu Kang has been here?"

"Yes, in November 1976 after the 'gang of four' was overthrown. She asked us to send a report to her."

So that was why Qin had been able to attend the National Science Conference! But why hadn't Liu mentioned this to me?

The light went out.

"There are sometimes electricity cuts so that the factories can use it. You must be tired after your trip. Better go and have a rest." He saw me to my room with a flashlight. "All the communes and brigades growing herbs love Qin. At the company's experimental plots even the old people and children know her. They say that Qin left her family behind to work here on this mountain. She first came as a young woman with dark glossy hair. Now she is going grey. We'll never forget what she's done for us."

In Qin's room, several young technicians were discussing their plans with her, and asking her questions about points they had not understood in the training class. They were returning to their brigades the following day.

Qin lit a candle for me and went back to her young people.

Tired out, I lay down on my bed. But sleep did not come. So I put the candle on an equipment box beside my bed, spread out the maps I'd borrowed from Wang and began copying them into my notebook.

Listening to the voices of Qin and the young people, my thoughts wandered.

I was thinking hard. What did a good relationship with the people mean? What was the criterion? Why did opinions about Qin differ so much?

Early the following morning, I strolled along the streets. I walked around the market-place, returned and stood at the gate of the medicinal herb company. The line of peasants selling herbs to the company kept growing. Company clerks were evaluating the herbs. Qin was there telling the clerks and the peasants how to distinguish real herbs from false ones, good from bad, and when to dig up a herb. . . . Qin, a university graduate, had become an expert in the study of medicinal herbs.

As Director Wang had arranged, we began visiting various old and new medicinal herb farms. Some were advanced, others mediocre or even backward.

As the car drove on, Wang told us how those farms had started and developed. Wherever we stopped, Qin always went to see the farm's technician first. Sometimes, she would tell me, "This is where my first year's experiment failed." Or, "When I first came here I made a fool of myself because I couldn't tell which herb was which."

Manglin Ridge, 1,800 metres above sea level, was now in sight. We were approaching Xiedi Production Brigade of Gucheng People's Commune. Little wooden and brick houses gradually appeared on the way. As we entered Xiedi Village, we heard a child's voice, sounding like a bird's chirp, "Aunty Qin!"

Blue sky. White clouds. Clumps of trees. Footpaths. Stone steps. Budding honeysuckle, red peonies in full bloom. A little girl, like a pink butterfly, fluttered down a hill slope and then threw herself into Qin's arms, crying out, "Aunty Qin, I saw you in my dream! Come to my home, hurry up!" The girl pushed Qin into her house. Then a small boy came and hugged her.

"Kangzheng, you've certainly grown fast! Oh look, you've got your shoes on the wrong way round." So saying, Qin sat down on a little stool, put the boy on her knee and changed his shoes.

Their mother, who had just returned from work in the fields for the noon break, handed us each a cup of sweet tea and then hastily took out dried persimmons and walnuts from the sideboard. She lit a fire and began preparing a meal, pouring out all her troubles in the process: how her husband, a brigade cadre, worked hard yet got snubbed; about her eldest son's girlfriend; her daughter's teacher; her mother; uncles.... She talked on and on until the medicinal herb farm manager came to take us to lunch.

"Why don't you have lunch here?" she said, rather put out. "I've already steamed the cakes."

"Too many people for you to cope with, sister," said the manager.

But she insisted, "They're Qin's friends. I don't mind even if I have to empty the rice pot."

It was not until after Qin explained we were really busy and promised to come back next time, she gave in. However, she wrapped up some dried persimmons in a clean handkerchief and stuffed it into Qin's bag. Qin left a package for her, in which were pencils and exercise books for the children. Since our hostess had told Qin that she had not been very well, Qin also gave her a prescription, so that she could go to the clinic to get some medicine. I had never imagined that Qin was so talented!

During lunch, the little girl slipped in and whispered something into Qin's ear, leaving a small basket of cakes for her.

I met many people in Xiedi Village and learned a lot. What Qin had done in this area became clear.

Xiedi Village was situated at the northern slope of the Manglin Mountains. All its fields and households were spread out on three northern sides of the mountains, four ridges, eight slopes and seven gullies. Though the peasants worked hard, their yield was pretty low. The land was poor and so were the people. But the mountains were fertile. The recognizable wild plants alone were well over a thousand. Red-rooted salvia had been growing for centuries over the slopes and ridges. The people living here did not know that its roots were in fact a precious medicine for curing heart disease. Young herdsmen would pluck its purple flowers and suck its honey. If a man was ill, he would travel fifty *li* to buy medicine at Gucheng where the commune headquarters were located. Yet right under their noses were all kinds of medicinal herbs. Later the county pharmaceutical company came down and bought dried salvia roots at a price of twenty *fen* a catty. After a few years, the purple flowers became rare like other wild medicinal herbs. In 1972, that company, in cooperation with Xi'an Botanical Gardens, began to cultivate medicinal herbs. Xi'an Botanical Gardens sent an experimental group, headed by the man who had once been in charge of "Qin Guanshu's Case", and Qin herself. Though "Qin Guanshu's Case" had been cleared by then, Qin was still in a difficult position. The peasants could tell that she had once been criticized for some "crime" and had been sent there "to reform herself". Nevertheless, they judged intellectuals and cadres, who were forced to work in the countryside, on their own merits.

Qin at first lived in a dilapidated temple. Early in the morning, she set out for the mountains taking with her some dried coarse food. Sometimes she could not find a drop of water all day. But she never complained. Her job was not easy, so the peasants began to think highly of her.

She was very responsible and diligent. She was so busy with her work that she could rarely go home to see her husband, son and daughter. Early in spring when the mountain slopes were not yet green she arrived. Even after the grass withered from the frost, the medicinal herbs had been collected and new seeds planted, she still remained. Sympathetic villagers often pressed her to go back home.

Before the group from Xi'an Botanical Gardens arrived, the villagers had attempted to cultivate elevated gastrodia, but it was a risky business for they lacked scientific knowledge. Thanks to the efforts of Qin and her colleagues, even children now knew how to grow it. At present, the medicinal herb farm run by the brigade grew one hundred and sixty elevated gastrodia. It was estimated that each could produce one to three catties of tubers. One catty could fetch six and a half yuan. In 1977, one elevated gastrodia yielded three and a half catties of tubers. No wonder the villagers said, "Science works!"

Qin experimented with ultrasonic waves on balloon-flower seeds which, consequently, sprouted fast.

Using the method of asexual reproduction, Qin cultivated red-rooted salvia on a large scale. The purple flowers covered the slopes. Even around the houses swarms of bees hummed about the clusters of flowers. The villagers said in delight, "We can exchange basketfuls of salvia tubers for a walking tractor!"

The medicinal herb farm, which originally had consisted of half a *mu* of peonies, had been enlarged to five hundred *mu*, of which three hundred grew woody plants.

From 1972 to 1977, the farm made a profit of 14,000 yuan, which covered the cost of the brigade's purchasing a tractor, a milling machine, threshers, barrows, sewing-machines and explosives for quarrying the mountains. In 1977, the farm produced 3,207 catties of medicinal

herbs and 250,000 seedlings.   It donated 3,200 catties
of medicinal seeds to other communes and villages. Its
contribution was even greater in 1978.   The red bean
yield alone, which could be used as both food and medicine, was estimated to be 10,000 catties, which could
be sold for 4,300 yuan.   The total income of the farm
was estimated to be 10,000 yuan.   Naturally, the villagers nicknamed the farm "the bank".

Though Qin did not often come here now, the villagers still knew that they owed much to her efforts and
knowledge.

For two days, there were always children following
Qin about, though they did not pester her.

"What will you do when you grow up?"   I asked
some children.

"We'll be like Aunty Qin," they replied.

So medicinal herbs were not the only things Qin had
nurtured.

The Manglin Mountains were steep and the paths
were slippery. I could manage to scramble up but found
it difficult to get down. The director of the farm made
me a bamboo stick.   Qin led us up a mountain, iden-
tifying cork trees, skullcap, eucommia, honeysuckle,
Chinese clematis, Gorgon fruit. . . .

During the visits, I felt that she was deliberately
avoiding me.   So I often tried to be near her on the
pretext of asking questions about herbs.   One day she
told me how to identify Chinese magnoliavine which,
she said, could help quench thirst if you could not find
any water.

She picked up a plant and asked me, "You know
this?"

It was probably some medicinal herb, but looked a

very ordinary weed. Its roots were like drumsticks. Judging from the little purple flowers I ventured, "Oh, God! Forget-me-not!"

With a grin, Qin said, "The name's not from God. It was perhaps given by a certain scholar living on a mountain centuries ago. Its name is narrow-leaved polygala, but the villagers just call it tiny weed or little weed. It can even grow in crevices in the rocks. The roots can be used as medicine, to help strengthen the mind. As western medicine puts it, it benefits the nerves of the brain." Looking serious now, she continued, "It is found all over the mountain, so there's no need to grow it. However, I've got a sample of it at home. When I've time, I take it out to look...."

I inquired, "In which university did you study this subject?"

This surprisingly annoyed her. "I've never studied it at all," she snapped, and then abruptly went down the mountain.

How could I find a way to her? I was at my wit's end. She was like a hurt pet, always on her guard. Did she suspect someone had told me something about her? Or rather did she fear that talking to me might lead to more trouble?

In the dusk before we left Xiedi, the girls crowded round me asking about life in cultural circles. I told them how our late premier, Zhou Enlai, had been concerned about intellectuals. To my astonishment, I noticed that Qin's face was flushed, her eyes full of tears.

One night when the rain pelted down outside, we two sat in a brick house, the newly built lab. In the dim candlelight, we recalled the days when Lin Biao and the "gang of four" were in power. We talked of the riot at Tiananmen Square in Beijing on April 5th, 1976.* Bit by bit, Qin told me what was preying on her mind.

Before Liberation, she quit school in the fifth form of middle school, for her big family was too poor to support her any more. So she became a teacher. In 1951, two years after Liberation, Qin, dreaming of afforesting the desert, sat an entrance examination to enter the Northwest Agricultural College. She was one of only two girl students in the faculty. When people advised her to transfer to some other department because of the tough conditions, she argued, "Don't worry! How do you know I won't be able to stand it?"

While still a student, she was greatly interested in poplar trees and did a lot of research on them. With the northern Shaanxi and Weishui River as the bases, together with some of her teachers and classmates, she made a study tour. Riding on horses, donkeys or camels, she went to Inner Mongolia and the Altai Mountains in Xinjiang. Finally she graduated with flying colours. In April 1959, when Xi'an Botanical Gardens were established, she went there to work. In 1961, she started introducing new species of poplar trees. Then she was made head of a research group.

In the gardens, there were more than a hundred species of poplars from all over the country.

Qin, accompanying some foreign botanists, visited the Emei and Taibai Mountains and the banks of the

---

* Referring to the mass demonstration against the "gang of four" for its suppression of popular activities commemorating Premier Zhou Enlai.

Weishui River. Later these scientists sent her some good strains of foreign poplar seeds.

Then the storm of the "cultural revolution" started. Qin became one of the main targets for attack and was dismissed from her work. Her research was stopped; her co-workers turned into enemies; the botanical gardens became a battlefield.

The best part of more than one hundred species of poplars were uprooted. The gardens were turned into fields for crops.

At the criticism meetings, Qin never admitted she had committed any "crime". Someone shouted at her, "The research on poplars is a revisionist subject, because it has nothing to do with production. Poplars have existed for thousands of years, what's the point of studying them? Every peasant knows how to grow a poplar!"

"Ignoramus!" Qin swore to herself in anger. She might be silent but never convinced. She was disheartened by a policy which could only hinder the development of science and technology.

Qin's heart ached to see that many good species of Chinese poplars had been dug up. She often strolled among the small foreign poplar trees. Though a strong-willed woman, she thought of suicide several times. The specimens she had collected over the years had been taken away; her notebooks had disappeared. Furious, she had sold her books, which she had bought with the money she had saved, as waste paper, or simply burnt them as kindling to light her stove. One morning, again she lit a fire with a book. It was not enough. Automatically she took another. But suddenly she jumped up, blankly looking at the book, her eyes filling with tears. She had never cried at the criticism meetings, but now, holding the torn book to her chest, she broke down.

The book was entitled *Report on the Problems Concerning Intellectuals*, a speech made by Premier Zhou at a conference sponsored by the Central Party Committee on January 14th, 1956. It had been given to her by the general branch of the Party committee of the Northwest Agricultural College.

After a long silence, I asked her, "It wasn't your wish to grow medicinal herbs, was it?"

"Of course not," she said frankly. "Why abandon my research work on poplars? Ridiculous! Besides, I had never studied medicine. When I was first asked to take part in the work of cultivating wild herbs, which they said was in preparation for war, I was worried. You know, I'm not from a good-class family. If it failed, they would put all the blame on me, saying I sabotaged it deliberately to avenge my class. How could I bear that? So I refused to go."

"Why did you change your mind later?"

She sighed, shaking her head. "When I was shut up illegally, I had to give up poplars. But once released, I wanted to work. Wasting time is an unbearable punishment. Someone said I was a complete revisionist, and that graduates of the past seventeen years could only sabotage socialism. I was determined to show them that I could do my bit for socialism. I did not blame the Party or the people. How could I have entered college without the Party? The people needed medicine. I was sure I could learn about it...."

After a pause, I asked her, "They say you're hot-tempered. Could you tell me about the worst time you lost your temper? And over what?"

She sat up abruptly and said, "It was when someone wanted to saw the small poplar trees, the only foreign species left in the gardens. That was when I had returned to Xi'an from the mountains. I found that someone wanted to destroy those little poplars. I stood before them and cried out, 'Why do you want to chop down these trees? You'll have to saw me first!' "

The candle burnt out, the room was pitch dark.

The rain had already stopped. The moon quietly showed itself, its light cascading through the treetops and silhouetting Qin's profile.

Qin continued, "Some kind-hearted people advised me not to get too het up over a few poplars. Why stand up to some people for the sake of a few trees? Of course it had nothing to do with me personally. It had not been easy for those poplars to acclimatize to our land. When they grew to maturity, their existence alone would be a scientific success. No one had the right to destory them!"

Her ? ?

On the way back to Xi'an, all I noticed, apart from peaks, ridges, rivers and dried river-beds, were poplars, big or small, flanking the several hundred kilometres long road. They seemed the only trees I could see on the slopes of the Qinling Mountains, which in reality were known for Chinese pines, oak and walnut trees. I could not distinguish which were the good poplars, but Qin's voice kept ringing in my ears, "If our country is widely planted with good poplars. . . ."

"Why did they stop the research on poplars?" I asked Liang, the Party secretary, though I knew he had not been transferred to the botanical gardens then. At that time he was being criticized in another place. However, he answered my question. "That research topic was given to the forestry institute."

"The first day I came, I heard, if I remember correctly, that Qin was forced to work on medicinal herbs, because that was not in her line. Do you think it was a wrong assignment?" I thought Liang had worked in an agricultural college before and knew what he was talking about.

"Let's put it this way," he said, "it's like an actor, acting this role today, playing another one tomorrow. It's not really a change of one's profession."

I shook my head. Though I had no idea how detailed plants could be classified, at least I could tell trees from herbs.

"She had studied in a college for four years, worked for six years, and her research was on poplars. Then suddenly she was told to drop this for medicine. For her it was a great change. It's like a film star or stage actor being asked to play a role in a Beijing opera. That's wrong!"

Liang explained, "It's quite normal to change one's work according to the needs of the botanical gardens."

"But can't you send Qin to a forestry institute?"

He countered hastily, "Huang Zongying, you mustn't encourage a brain drain!"

I said laughing, "She wouldn't give up her medicinal

herbs now even if you tried to force her!" Then I asked, "What about that tree felling incident?"

"What trees?"

"The small foreign poplar trees. Did Qin have a row with somebody over it?"

"She's hot-tempered and she's got a sharp tongue."

"But was she right?"

"Sometimes she's right. But she ought to be more tactful in her dealings with others. Once some people were building a shed among the poplars. Suddenly she appeared, yelling that the smoke from the chimney would ruin the trees. We called a meeting and decided to move the shed."

It was true. Qin had told me that Liang had called an urgent meeting for that.

"But what about felling the poplars?" I insisted.

"We just wanted to reduce the density of the trees. After a year of planting, sometimes the inside of a tree changes its colour. That means they're too densely planted."

I was silent. If what he said was true, then Qin had made a fuss over nothing.

I asked one of her colleagues, "What do you think of Qin's work in the mountains?"

"She was tough and hard-working. It's true Luonan County did a very good job in cultivating wild herbs. But we can't owe it all to Qin alone. Besides, it can hardly be called scientific research. Many places have done the same. Even peasants can do it."

"What about using ultrasonic waves on seeds? Isn't that a scientific achievement?" I thought of Qin's index cards, which were full of notes, records of experiments and so on. I also remembered the article published in the name of the Scientific Group, Xi'an Botanical Gardens.

"That's a very common method."

I asked another man, "Was the criticism of Qin correct? Do you think it was overdone?"

The reply was: "We didn't play rough here. Nobody ever raised a finger to her. At most, she was asked to wear a white band round her arm, criticized at several meetings, held in detention for a short period of time. Of course she did some hard labour. After all it was a big campaign. She should have a correct attitude towards it."

"How would you carry out the Party's policies towards someone who had once been illegally detained?"

He found it a strange question and said, "Carry out the Party's policies towards her? Wasn't she sent to Beijing to attend the conference? Besides, no one has ever made any conclusion about her case, nor has anyone put anything into her file. After all she's not perfect. She. . . ."

I also asked the man who had been leading "Qin Guanshu's Case", "Is Qin really from a landlord's family?"

He replied seriously, "It's something one can't change. According to the form the local government filled in when she entered college, she's from a landlord's family. . . . I sent people to check again. Her class origin's certain."

"Qin told me that the local government had never said that her father was a landlord."

"Everybody wants to defend himself, I suppose."

"Everybody wants to defend himself!" I repeated.

God! In the world of plants, no two leaves have the same pattern of veins. But in the world of human beings, people have to be classified and tagged all over the country. But how can these tags express the complications of Chinese society? After all, class origin is not terribly important.

I asked another comrade, "I think the leaders of Xi'an Botanical Gardens have always supported Qin's work, haven't they?"

"Not enough. But on the whole ... they supported her."

"Why then do they keep changing her technicians, co-workers and assistants?"

"Qin's bad-tempered. Besides, she doesn't behave so well in her personal life. A young technician and she hit it off well. But ... she. ..."

My heart sank. Qin was simple and honest. ...

"How old was he?" I asked.

"Twenty-five or six."

"How could it be possible?" My heart contracted.

"But it's true that she introduced him to her daughter. He's probably her son-in-law now."

I was wide-eyed in astonishment and demanded, "But what's wrong with that? What's wrong with that?"

"People don't like it. There's a lot of gossip going on!"

Oh God!

Finally I asked Liang, "Tell me, should I write about Qin or not?"

"Go ahead. It's your right."

"Quite a number of people in your gardens have

opinions about her. Will it make things worse if I write about her?"

"It doesn't matter. We'll make them understand. After all, it's only talk. At present, people are just too busy to care about such things."

I also asked some other people, "You didn't agree to send Qin to the National Science Conference, did you?"

Some replied, "Yes, we did."

Others answered, "Someone had to go, but it was wrong to set her up as a model and ask us to learn from her!"

"Should I write about her?" I did not know whether I was asking myself or the Party secretary.

Another Sunday. But to us writers, it did not make much difference. I had learned something new, and there were more questions in my mind. My political understanding was low; my logic poor. I was not able to make out what they meant. Nevertheless, Qin had left a deep impression on me in Luonan. I wanted to write about her.

I thought and thought until my head ached. Then I forced myself to read a book on plants. Like a student, I read while jotting down some notes.

Suddenly Liu Kang appeared. "It's Sunday," she said. "Why on earth bury your head in books? Come on! Have some fun at my home. You're not to do any work today. Nor do we talk seriously." Then she dragged me away.

Chatting while cracking sunflower seeds and drinking tea, I forgot Qin temporarily. Then I picked up the topic of Qin without realizing it. When I said, "Qin stood before a poplar tree and shouted, 'Who dares chop it down? You'll have to saw me first!'" Liu stood up abruptly and exclaimed, "Good for her! Good we have such women! We know too little about her." I thought she knew Qin quite well. Otherwise, how could Qin have attended the conference in Beijing when she was still in a difficult position? But why didn't Liu mention the fact that she had visited the mountains?

"Someone said that the trees must be felled to reduce the density," I carried on.

"Oh?" Liu said. "On a problem like that, I think Qin's the most authoritative person in Xi'an Botanical Gardens."

"There are many contradictions," I said, "I hope I can have an opportunity to talk to the Provincial Commission of Science and Technology."

"Yang Ge's the person to go to. I'll fix an appointment for you."

As soon as I met Yang, he said to me, "As for felling poplar trees to reduce the density, it's nonsense. The leaders of the botanical gardens had decided it. They needed some wood because they were building houses. So Qin was right. Liang admitted it too. Qin is a woman of principle."

I told him, "Generally speaking, to praise advanced people is one of the purposes of reportage. Qin's case is already beyond its scope. I suggest that you send a group to do some investigation work. For instance, was Qin's father a landlord?"

"Even if she's from a landlord's family," he said, "why can't she be written about? It's she who counts,

Suppose she's from a landlord's family, so what? She's not her father!"

I added, "Of course, many intellectuals have had a complicated background. Shortly after Liberation, her father was appointed the director of a local forestry bureau. He was also made vice-chairman of the local Chinese Political Consultative Conference. He was a professional. Her mother was a Zhuang serf. Qin's younger brother and sister, who were only one or two years her junior, claimed that they were from a professional family. So why is Qin tagged as from a landlord's family? During the 'cultural revolution', her father was dismissed and sent back to his home village. When he became seriously ill, Qin brought him back to town and he died at her house. So this became her principal crime."

Yang thought for some time and then said, "I think you'd better write as you want. Be bold! You heard what the peasants and local cadres said about her; you saw how hard she worked in the village. As for her class origin, we'll help you to find it out. Do you still have some hesitations?"

"I'll certainly write about her even if her father was a war criminal! But I must know some more facts. In her family, seven people have worked in forestry. You know, one of the first people who became engaged in it was Qin's husband. It's not an easy job. 'Landlord!' Are the Qins all so eager to work in forestry so that they can take over the bare mountains and deserts? Do they want to be the owners of the forests?" I poured out all my anger and frustrations. My voice grow louder, as if I was quarrelling with someone. Yang did not mind. He smiled. "Carry on! Write it up! We'll support you. Don't worry."

I'm neither cowardly, nor dauntless. My job is to write for society. Of course, Qin was not perfect. But who is?

Qin still remained vague, unclear. Though I had already filled a notebook, it was like a tangled mess of threads.

During the "cultural revolution", I came to know a lot about myself and others. When someone mentioned a name, others would say immediately, "Oh, I know him." Did they really know him? No. Their knowledge was derived from the big-character posters, tabloids and criticism meetings. And there were so many cases where there was no clear verdict; so much hearsay. The problems of class origin, identification and so on were passed on from mouth to mouth, yet no one bothered to find out the truth. So they stuck. The people in Xi'an Botanical Gardens had no real prejudice against Qin, but their minds had been poisoned, thanks to the ten years of chaos.

I planned to finish writing this when the wild-geese returned from the north. However, hesitation delayed my pen. Should I write about contradictions? Would the reportage be published? Would it solve the problems? Qin had been to Beijing to attend the conference. Her case was certainly better than many other intellectuals whose problems still remained. If it was no longer typical, this was good news. I dreamed of seeing the wild-geese hovering, circling outside my window. They perched in a semi-circle round my desk, looking at my manuscript. I heard a gander say, "Ah — that's very common, very common. We often see such cases on our way from north to south and south to north. Very often!"

The others urged, "Solve their problems! Hurry! Hurry!"

They took away my manuscript, each bird holding in its beak a sheet of paper. In a V formation, they flew away, far, far away....

Translated by Yu Fanqin and Wang Mingjie

Zong Pu in 1980

Zong Pu

ZONG Pu, born in Beijing in 1928, is the daughter of Feng Youlan, author of a history of Chinese philosophy. Her family evacuated to Kunming during the War of Resistance Against Japan; but during those turbulent years she had a good education and solid grounding in literature. After graduating from Qinghua University, in the '60s she worked on the editorial boards of the *Literary Gazette* and *World Literature*. She has written many stories and essays. Her "Melody in Dreams", printed in 1980, embodies her personal experience of the persecution of intellectuals during the "cultural revolution", and the courage of the young people who in 1976 went to Tiananmen Square to mourn for Premier Zhou Enlai and protest against the feudal fascism of the "gang of four". She now works in the Foreign Literature Research Institute of the Academy of Social Sciences. She is also a member of the Chinese Writers' Association.

Melody in Dreams

Zong Pu

MURONG Yuejun, a teacher of the cello at a music college, was wedded to her instrument. She and her cello were as one, and playing it she could express all her feelings. This day, however, she could not finish any piece. Putting the cello aside, she walked on to the balcony and gazed into the distance.

It was September 1975. In the setting sun a strand of her white hair gleamed. Although she was over fifty, her face was still attractive. She gazed at the end of the street, expecting a girl to appear, but no one came. This was the daughter of her close friend Liang Feng, whom she had nearly married. Although he had since died, she remained fond of his daughter.

On the outbreak of the Anti-Japanese War in 1937, Liang Feng and other youths had gone to Yan'an, the revolutionary base. Yuejun, however, who was a music student at Yanjing University in Beijing at the time, had been taken by her parents to the south. Then she had won a scholarship to study abroad and had not returned until after Liberation in 1949. After the death of her parents, she had immersed herself in teaching music.

Now it was growing dark. She went back into her room thinking.

In the first years after Liberation Liang Feng had worked abroad. In the sixties he had been recalled to China to do cultural exchange work. Yuejun had heard him speak at some meetings. She was impressed by his way of expounding the Party's policies and moved by his devotion to the Party. She even met his wife, a good comrade and kind mother.

Yuejun had met their daughter, but the girl had not left a deep impression on her, except on one unforgettable occasion. It was during the "cultural revolution", when all sorts of bad characters emerged to slander celebrated artists and intellectuals. Yuejun, because she had studied abroad, was attacked. At a meeting, she and some others were lined up on a stage. Some famous musicians were pushed to the microphone to denounce themselves as reactionaries. Suddenly three or four youngsters beat and kicked a middle-aged man on to the stage shouting: "Down with the revisionist monster Liang Feng!"

Stealing a glance at him, Yuejun was surprised to see her friend being forced to the microphone. Facing the crowd, he said: "I'm Liang Feng, a Chinese Communist!"

No sooner had he said this when some thugs leapt on to the platform and punched him. Blood poured from his mouth. Then a girl's clear voice was heard shouting: "Father! Father!"

There was an uproar as some protested against the beating, while others rushed to the girl and kicked her out of the hall. Though Yuejun's head was lowered, she saw the whole scene, except for the girl's face. Whenever she thought of her, she felt a mixture of sadness and warmth.

Now she was expecting her.

There was a voice outside. Yuejun asked: "Is that you, Pei?" A plump woman of Yuejun's age entered, a Party committee member in her department.

A bosom friend of Yuejun, she said: "I just popped in to see if Liang Feng's daughter was coming to see you today."

"She's supposed to, but she hasn't turned up yet."

"Do you remember. . . ?" Pei looked out of the window.

"I haven't forgotten all those slanders." Yuejun's mild glance rested on her. After each criticism meeting, Pei had whispered in her ear: "Chin up! It's a test." Or: "Never mind. Don't let it upset you too much!" This had enormously encouraged Yuejun.

Pei had high blood pressure and was easily excited. Controlling herself she said: "You must teach her well, Yuejun."

"Of course. I want to, but could I supplement the material?"

"I think one should, but who has the authority? The bad people aren't only trying to destroy the good ones, but also our whole civilization and socialism." Pei's voice quivered.

"But what can we do?" Yuejun mutttered.

"Wait until. . . ." Pei slapped the arm of the armchair. After a while she said she was going to see her paralysed husband in the hospital. Smiling bitterly, she left.

It was night as Yuejun gazed out of the window at the maple tree illuminated by neighbouring lights. Thinking of the girl, she supposed she wouldn't come that night. Then there was a knock at the door.

Before she could answer it, a girl came in saying loudly: "Are you Aunt Yuejun? I had such trouble in finding your home, I must have asked about a dozen people the way. Your room's dark but I spotted your cello when I came in, so I guessed this must be the right place. I'm Liang Xia."

Switching on the lights, Yuejun saw that Liang Xia was a pretty girl, with her hair cut short. She was wearing a cream-coloured jacket over a black woollen jersey, and deep grey trousers. With large eyes, slender eyebrows and rosy cheeks, she was smiling quizzically at Yuejun.

"So she's sizing me up too," thought Yuejun, who shook hands with her, saying: "I've been waiting for you. . . ."

2

Liang Xia was nineteen. She was ten years old in 1966 when the "cultural revolution" had begun and this marked a turning-point in her life. Until then she had been the pride of the parents, but her happiness had fled with the start of the "cultural revolution". Since her father had been a leader of his office, one night some people broke into their home and dragged him away. Then her mother was separated from her. Liang Xia, bewildered, was alone at home, cooking meals to take to her parents. Her father liked eating noodles and flapjacks, while her mother liked sweet food. Sometimes because Liang Xia hadn't cooked enough food, she herself went hungry in order to give her parents their meals. She did this until one day a man told her not to prepare any more for her father, since he had died five days earlier.

After her parents were detained, some of their comrades invited Liang Xia to live with them, but certain people objected saying that she could only live with a relative. She had an aunt, her mother's sister, but she had refused to take Liang Xia, only allowing the girl to visit her and help her with various chores. At that time Liang Xia was in the fourth-grade at school. Because of her parents, she too was criticized from time to time.

In those unhappy days, Liang Xia often dreamed she was being weighed down by a heavy stone. Unable to remove it she would cry herself awake. But in time she became accustomed to the sneers, and hid the hatred in her heart. After her mother's release, her mother was sent to a cadre school to do manual labour and took her there. Then her mother was transferred to work in a small town in south China, where she met a cello teacher, who had been dismissed from his school. So that Liang Xia wouldn't idle away her time, her mother arranged for her to have cello lessons. Two months previously, her mother had died of illness. This was tragic because it was said there would soon be a meeting to clear her husband's name. Liang Xia came to Beijing and stayed with her aunt. She hoped that Yuejun could give her cello lessons. That was the reason for her visit.

"I'm sorry for being late, but I had to help my aunt with the washing up." She glanced round the room in which Yuejun had lived for many years. Against the window was a marble-topped mahogany desk left to Yuejun by her parents. At one corner stood a piano against which leant a cello. In front of her bed was a folding screen painted with flowers and birds. Two armchairs flanked a stand, behind which was a lamp with an orange shade. The gentle light gave an atmosphere of tranquillity.

"It's nice and cosy here," Liang Xia said as she followed Yuejun to the kitchen, where she took the thermos flask from her and poured herself a cup of tea. "We were driven out of our home and had to leave everything," she said matter-of-factly. "When my parents were detained, I stayed in the attic. It seemed quite cosy at the time. But mother was ill after her release and whenever she used the stairs I had to carry her on my back."

Yuejun wondered how Liang Xia, with her delicate build, had managed that. Curious to know about her mother's illness, Yuejun nevertheless said nothing in case she opened old wounds.

But as if she had read her thoughts, Liang Xia continued: "Mother had all sorts of complaints. I was like her doctor. I knew every medicine she took. In the end she died of pneumonia. I thought many times she would die, but she always survived. So I thought she'd recover that last time." Her tone seemed detached. Yuejun, however, was very sad.

"How many years have you been playing the cello?" Yuejun looked at her cello. "You love music, don't you?"

"No, I don't." Her reply surprised Yuejun, who stared fascinated at her thick lashes and dark eyes. "I have to learn something to get myself a job. I've been playing since I was fourteen, but I'm not interested in it. I really preferred working in the countryside, but since my mother was too ill to join me, I went with her."

Yuejun was disappointed and wondered whom Liang Xia would follow now.

The girl added: "My parents were always talking about you, so I feel as if I've known you for ages. Mother said you could help me to become a musician." A flicker of hope came into her eyes veiling the indifference which seemed to say: "Anyway, it doesn't matter if you refuse."

"Why bother learning to play the cello if you don't like it?"

"To make a living of course," Liang Xia giggled.

If she had heard such a reply ten years ago, Yuejun would have been insulted. Now nothing astonished her.

"Play me something," she said after a pause.

When Liang Xia went to take the cello, she found a curtained-off recess behind which Yuejun stored her junk. Lifting the curtain, Liang Xia exclaimed: "Goodness! Why do you store away all your things here, auntie? One day I'll help you sort them out." Then holding the cello she began to play.

She played the second movement of a concerto by Saint-Saëns. In spite of her poor technique, there was something moving in her playing which touched Yuejun. Although she failed to grasp the meaning of the music, she expressed her own feelings. She was making music.

"She has a good musical sense," Yuejun thought.

Although she soon finished, the room was filled with the atmosphere she had created. Putting aside the cello, Liang Xia searched Yuejun's face.

"To have a feeling for the music is most important,"

Yuejun said warmly. "But you don't handle your bow correctly yet. Look, it should be like this," and so saying she took the bow and gave the girl her first lesson.

3

After that, Liang Xia came once a week. When she wasn't studying, she'd chat or help Yuejun with something. She was bright and seemed to know a lot, though sometimes she was ignorant of the most common knowledge. For example, once a colleague was discussing some classical novels with Yuejun, when Liang Xia interrupted them saying she had read many of them. It seemed she had read whatever she could lay her hands on, but there were very large gaps in her education. She may have seemed self-centred, knowing how to take care of herself, because since the death of her parents no one had shown any concern for her. She sometimes, however, was ready to help others.

One day Yuejun was learning to give injections. Liang Xia offered her arm because she said she wasn't afraid of pain. Then she added coolly: "Trouble is, you're afraid because you haven't been beaten up enough!" She seemed to have seen through everything and scorned the glowing revolutionary jargon in the newspapers. She would say: "All lies! Even Premier Zhou was slandered as a reactionary. Who's foolish enough to swallow that!" Her only belief was that Premier Zhou would triumph over those "bastards". Yuejun hoped the same.

When she referred to Jiang Qing, she called her a "she-devil" who had created so many scandals and who still tried to fool the people. "She praises a novel about vengeance, while she really intends to attack us. One day I'll take my revenge on her!" Her words puzzled Yuejun. She spoke freely, not caring about the situation. At times Yuejun was afraid lest she should get into trouble.

Pei, a frequent visitor, soon got to know Liang Xia well enough to make her drop her pose of flippancy and talk seriously.

One day Pei came to hear Liang Xia play. After listening to her she asked Yuejun, "If you want to supplement your teaching material, why not use some Western études? You're too timid, I think."

Bow in hand, Liang Xia protested: "Of course she's timid, but what about you?"

"I never said I was bold," Pei smiled, "but we've each got a head on our shoulders, and we should use our brains to find ways and means."

"My head's too heavy for me. I don't like it. If you want, Aunt Pei, I'll give it to you. Then you'll be bold enough to make revolution. Only don't get scared because you'll have to turn everything upside-down." She burst out laughing. "Revolution sounds fine but they murdered my father under that name also!"

"No, that was counter-revolutionary," Pei burst out. "Stop playing the fool and remember what your mother said to you. Remember those who hounded your father to death. You must think seriously about your future."

Liang Xia immediately became grave, bit her lip and stared at Pei. After a moment she lapsed into her usual flippancy and sneered: "I don't give a fig for them! What about dinner? Let's go and make it. I'm quite good at cooking. . . ." She laughed.

That was how she had reacted.

Once when Yuejun asked about her future plans, she answered as briefly as before, adding with a movement of her eyebrows: "I'll fool around until my aunt throws me out, but that won't be immediately. She knows that my father's name may be cleared and that she stands to gain." Then she went to the recess and lifting the curtain looked at it again.

Before long her aunt turned her out. It was on an early winter day, when Liang Xia should have arrived for her lesson. At sunset she still hadn't come. Yuejun wondered in concern what had happened to her.

Suddenly Liang Xia burst in, a bulky satchel over her shoulder and a string bag in her hand. With a face flushed with rage, she cried: "Sorry to keep you waiting, but I've just had a hell of a row with my aunt." Then putting down her bags in a corner, she sat down fanning herself with a handkerchief. Her eyes burned with resentment as she jeered and laughed: "It's just ridiculous!"

"Don't laugh like that," Yuejun said patting Liang Xia's shoulder. "Tell me what happened."

"My aunt said that my father's name can't be cleared because he was a reactionary and that he had killed himself to escape punishment. As for me, since I'm his daughter there's no future for me. My staying with her has caused her a lot of trouble. Since her husband is going to be made a deputy-minister and their block of flats is for ministers, ordinary people like me shouldn't be living there. We're a security risk. What rot!"

Yuejun sympathized with her and wondered what she would do next.

"I'll stay with you, if I may? You aren't afraid?" she asked standing up.

Yuejun was silent. Of course she was afraid! To let Liang Xia stay with her could mean she too would be labelled as a counter-revolutionary. But how could she push her out? After all, she was Liang Feng's daughter.

Seeing Yuejun's hesitation, Liang Xia smiled with scorn. Then she noticed that she had reached a decision. Before Yuejun could say anything, Liang Xia walked over to the curtained recess and put her things by it. "I've thought about it before. We can put a bed here." As she spoke she began pulling out the junk. "You sit over there, auntie." She sneezed. "So much dust! I always said I'd help you spring-clean it one day. Now my words have come true!" She laughed delightedly.

Despite the dust she hummed a tune as she worked. Having finished cleaning, she arranged the things in two piles of boxes and cases, on which she placed some planks for a bed. Then she made it up with sheets and a quilt lent to her by Yuejun. With a board from the kitchen she made herself a desk. Among the junk she had found a tattered scroll on which was written a poem. This read:

> Coming from your old home,
> You should know what is happening there;
> Outside the silk screened window,
> Did you see the plums in blossom?

Holding it in her hands, Liang Xia softly read it twice.

"Who wrote it?" she asked. "Both the poem and the calligraphy are good. Why don't you hang it up?"

"Wouldn't that be criticized?" Yuejun replied joking. "It was only this year that I put my screen here. Honestly I'm afraid of courting trouble."

"Well, I'm not." Examining it, Liang Xia noticed the inscription: "A poem by Wang Wei copied by Yuejun in G. city." The girl exclaimed: "So you wrote it! No wonder the calligraphy's so good." Immediately she hung it above her bed. Stepping back she gazed at it and then, clapping her hands, asked: "But where's G. city?"

"Geneva, in Switzerland." Yuejun looked at the old writing with some emotion. "I was there alone studying music and I felt very homesick. Once I listened to Dvorak's *New World Symphony* a dozen times non-stop. Whenever it reached the second movement I was deeply moved. So I wrote that poem on the scroll. What awful calligraphy!"

"There's patriotism in your words." Liang Xia gave a bitter smile. "Now even patriotism is getting criticized."

"I didn't have any clear ideas." Yuejun sat down at the table. "But I truly missed China then. My ancestors and I had been born here. I was proud to be Chinese. That's why I appreciated that short poem. But if that is all wrong now, what's left?" Moodily she turned to the window: "Of course I learned Western music, but only so that I could serve my country better."

"Your country?" Liang Xia mocked. "Today that means individualism, egotism and counter-revolutionary revisionism!" Then she laughed. "Anyway you're all right as a musician. Isn't singing and acting coming into fashion?"

Yuejun didn't want to comment on her harsh words:

At last Liang Xia had finished tidying up. "My bed's rather like a raft, isn't it?" Going over to it she said: "I'll stay on my raft. I'll be as quiet as a mouse in the day." Having climbed on to her "raft" she suddenly popped her head out of the curtain and quipped: "Carefree on my raft, I don't mind whether the seasons come or go." Then she was quiet.

"Now there's no need to act like that," Yuejun laughed. Drawing back the curtain, she found that Liang Xia was lying back on her quilt, her eyes closed. On her rosy cheeks were streaks of dirt. "Get up and wash your face, Liang Xia. We'll have a lesson. Since you'll be staying here for a while, you mustn't waste your time."

On hearing her say "for a while", Liang Xia smiled faintly and glanced sadly at her.

At half-past eight that evening they had a lesson. Liang Xia played first. Her technique was improving. As Yuejun was correcting her, there was a knock at the door.

A youngster in a green uniform without any insignia entered. The expression on his regular-featured face was troubled. Seeing Liang Xia sitting with the cello in her hands, he said to Yuejun: "Excuse me, are you Aunt Yuejun? I'd like to have a word with her." Then he smiled at Liang Xia.

Ignoring him, Liang Xia concentrated on her music, but after a while she explained: "This is Mao Tou. A friend of my cousin. Let's continue our lesson."

"Mao Tou? Is that a nickname?" asked Yuejun casually, wondering about their relationship.

"Actually I don't know his real name." With this Liang Xia continued playing.

Snubbed, the young man turned to Yuejun for help. She suggested, looking at Liang Xia, that they go for a walk in the fresh air. Then she went to her desk and switched on the lamp. Pouting Liang Xia slouched out with her friend.

The next day at school, Yuejun told Pei about her decision. The latter was delighted. "I agree with you. She should live in your home." Some colleagues who sympathized with Liang Xia felt in this way she could have an opportunity to study, as she'd become an orphan and a loafer. "But who'll be responsible for her?" Pei asked. Those who objected said: "What if the police start making inquiries? And if Liang Xia does something illegal, Yuejun will be implicated." Yuejun was worried, but decided that if the authorities insisted the girl should leave, then she must do so. Otherwise Liang Xia could stay as long as she liked.

Time passed, and Yuejun and Liang Xia got on well together. The latter was able, diligent and considerate. Always in high spirits, she reminded Yuejun of an elf from a dance by Grieg. But Liang Xia claimed to be a very down-to-earth sort of person. "If you were me," she argued, "you'd be just as practical."

The weather grew chilly and Yuejun bought Liang Xia some cloth intending to have a jacket made at the tailor's. But Liang Xia took it and said she could make it herself. She went to Pei's home where there was a sewing-machine. On her return, she looked grave.

"What's the matter?" Yuejun asked.

"Oh, nothing!" Liang Xia fidgeted with the remnants of the cloth. "Aunt Pei's husband's been paralysed for three years, and she has to go to the hospital every day to take care of him. Though she has high blood pressure, she still goes to her office and studies the works of Marx and Lenin. She told me that in the Yan'an days, she wore straw sandals yet every step she took seemed significant. Life was so full of hope. There she became friends with my parents." After a moment her face brightened and she continued: "Aunt Pei said my father helped to reclaim the waste land and that my mother spun yarn. I'd like to live such a life, but now even playing my cello's illegal." Scissors in hand, she shredded the cloth.

Her usual apathetic and scornful expression returned, her tender heart seemed to have hardened. As Yuejun stroked her silky black hair, there was a knock at the door. Two young men with high sheepskin hats and fashionable trousers entered. Seeing them, Liang Xia sprang forward and told them to get out, banging the door shut. Her friends annoyed Yuejun, who didn't know where Liang Xia picked them up. If she was at home, then Liang Xia would take them out, but while she was teaching or elsewhere, Yuejun was quite ignorant of what went on in her home. As most of them were boys, she once tentatively warned Liang Xia against falling in love too early.

Hearing this, Liang Xia burst out laughing. "Don't worry! I shan't be such a fool! I don't respect those boys. When I marry, he'll be a high official!" She grinned pulling a face, as if in her eyes high officials were toys for amusement. Then affecting gravity, she added: "Or perhaps I'll be a spinster like you. By the way, why didn't you marry, aunt?"

"You tell me," Yuejun countered trying to avoid the question.

"It isn't that you believe in being single, but that you've never met a man you loved." She was sharp.

Since her arrival, Yuejun had been strict in making her practise various pieces every day. Though she did not assign any Western musical scores, Liang Xia often played some to amuse herself. One day when Yuejun returned, she overheard Liang Xia playing a plaintive melody by Massenet. It was so melancholy that she waited till Liang Xia had finished before entering.

Yuejun often wished that Liang Xia could attend a proper school, since she had real musical talent. But it all depended on when her father's name would be cleared. If that happened, then the girl would be in a better position to study.

Meanwhile Liang Xia led a seemingly carefree life. Apart from playing the cello and seeing friends, she often read some books on her "raft". One day Yuejun was shocked to find her reading a hand-written copy of an "underground" book. "Why are you reading that?" she asked.

"Why not?" Liang Xia retorted.

"The cover alone scares me."

"You wouldn't even say boo to a goose!" Liang Xia giggled. "When my parents were detained I was often criticized and beaten. Later I fought the boys back. They beat me and I punched them. I loved it!"

Not knowing what to say, Yuejun stared at her pretty, youthful face. Despite the merry, contemptuous expression, she sensed hidden apathy and misery.

"Since I'm older now, I've grown out of fighting. It bores me." Then she tried to reassure Yuejun: "Please don't worry, auntie. But I can't play the cello all day long. I must read some books too. Since I can't find any good ones, I'm reading these, even though they're bad. It's like food. When there's nothing delicious, I eat anything. So there!" She glanced at the cabinet in which were locked some good books.

"You're wrong." Yuejun tried to argue against her.

"I know." Smiling she added: "Now I just exist. If one day I can't go on like this, then I'll change my world outlook. That's how Mao Tou puts it."

"You can read what he's read, I think." Yuejun had found that Mao Tou was a thoughtful young man who had studied seriously some books on philosophy, literature and history. Although known as a "scholar" in his factory, he refused to join any writing teams run by the authorities. His father was an old cadre, who had often shown concern for Liang Xia.

Yuejun's suggestion made Liang Xia smile again. After a moment, Yuejun opened the cabinet to let her choose whatever book she wanted. Happily Liang Xia looked through it until she suddenly murmured: "My father had many books. However late he worked he never went to bed before he had read a little. What a pity I was so young! I . . . I hate. . . ." Turning round she clutched hold of the cabinet, her eyes blazing. "Oh father! Father!" Her voice was as clear and pained as a few years before. "I don't believe that my father, a Communist full of enthusiasm, committed suicide. They killed him, but insist that he killed himself." She didn't choose a book, but stood there gazing wisefully at Yuejun. "Do you think the day I long for will come? Mother told me I must live to see it."

Yuejun couldn't bear to see her expression. Wanting Liang Xia to have a good cry, tears began pouring down her own face. Even if her father had killed himself, he would never have done so unless driven to it. He must have been in a terrible situation. She wanted to cry with Liang Xia hoping the girl's tears would wash away her cynicism. Instead Liang Xia rushed to her bed, leaving on the cabinet two snicks from her nails.

4

It was 1976 and the Spring Festival was approaching. Despite the festival, everyone was grieving. Where was the spring? People were profoundly anxious about their future since the death of Premier Zhou. There was a dreadful abyss in their hearts, which could not be filled by their tears and thoughts.

Before she went to the cadre school in January to do some manual labour, Yuejun entrusted Liang Xia to Pei's care. When she heard the sad news of the premier's death, she felt desolate. Worried that something might happen to Liang Xia, she wrote to her asking how she was. After she had posted the letter, Yuejun was afraid lest Liang Xia reply in an incautious way, so she quickly sent a message telling her not to answer. However, her reply came. It said: "I'm prepared to shoulder my responsibilities now." Though cryptic, it signified that a storm was imminent.

On her return home, Yuejun found Liang Xia had changed. She seldom talked and never laughed in that old distressing way. She thought more about her responsibilities. Sometimes Yuejun told her to play her cello to find peace in the music, but thinking about Premier Zhou disturbed her playing. In the past three weeks she had suddenly matured. Her flippancy had gone. In her dark eyes was a clouded expression, since her thoughts seemed too heavy to convey. Some of her friends stopped coming, since they were just playmates. When asked by Yuejun where her friends were, Liang Xia blinked as if she had never known them.

She had got rid of those frivolous books, but she was not interested in serious literature either. To Yuejun's surprise, Liang Xia sometimes read works of Marx and Lenin. On the eve of the Spring Festival, Pei found her reading an article by Chairman Mao, a notebook by her side. Leafing through its pages, Pei was astonished to find a heading: "Crimes perpetrated by Jiang Qing." The charges listed were logical and cogent. Pei grasped Liang Xia's hand and said admiringly: "I always thought you were a fine girl, Xia!"

Liang Xia smiled a genuine smile. "I thought a long time about your advice. I shouldn't fritter away my life and youth. Especially at this time."

Most of the notes had been made by Liang Xia and some by Mao Tou. As Yuejun read them, she felt they were telling the truth. But the truth meant trouble. She searched Pei's face wanting to know what to do.

Pei smiled at her. "It's correct to expose them for what they are. These notes are what we've been wanting to say ourselves."

Liang Xia told Yuejun: "I know that's the way you feel too. But you are too timid, auntie."

Yuejun sighed: "To whom could we speak?"

"We're only allowed to parrot the editorials," Pei added.

Liang Xia was silent. Her smile faded into contempt and pessimism.

Yuejun anxiously looked at the girl, while Pei warned: "It isn't just a question of daring to struggle.

It's also knowing how and when to strike."

After a quick supper in the dim light, Yuejun wanted to ask Liang Xia why she and Mao Tou had written these notes, but she didn't press her.

Suddenly there were three knocks at the door. Liang Xia immediately darted to open it and Mao Tou entered. Although he looked tense, he didn't forget his manners, greeting Yuejun before turning to Liang Xia. "Let's go out," he suggested.

"What's the matter?"

"Please sit down," Yuejun urged. "It's so cold outside. Don't go out. Tell us what's happened."

Eyeing them both, he said: "My father's been arrested!"

"What?" Yuejun was dismayed.

"On what charge?" Liang Xia asked.

"They can trump up anything," he replied, trying to control his anger. Then he continued: "A few days ago, my father told me they were concocting some charge against Premier Zhou. He said as long as he was alive he'd defend him and speak out. This morning your uncle told my father that they wanted him to attend a meeting. A neighbour reported that my father was bundled into his car. He wasn't even allowed to leave a note for the family."

"I was luckier. I saw my father being dragged away," Liang Xia murmured.

"When I went to their office to see my father, the man on duty told me coldly that he's to stand trial and wouldn't let me see him. Then he shoved me out of the door."

Yuejun was outraged thinking how many families had been ruined by the gang; how many young people had been deprived of their right to work and study or even lost their lives. They wouldn't even leave the premier alone. Our great hero had left nothing of himself after his death. Even his ashes had been scattered over the mountains and rivers. Now they intended to blacken his reputation.

Liang Xia trembled with rage. She suddenly laughed aloud. Yuejun took her hand which felt cold. "Xia!" she exclaimed.

"Those monsters are about to tear off their masks!" Brushing Yuejun aside, she put one hand on the table and the other to her breast.

"Yes, I think they are going to show their true intentions soon," said Mao Tou, looking coolly at Liang Xia. "We must continue collecting our material. The day's coming when the gang will be brought to trial and condemned."

"If my father were alive today, he'd do as yours has done, I'm sure."

Mao Tou paced the room and then said he was going to inform his friends about his father's arrest. He left after shaking hands with Yuejun and warning her to be careful.

At the door Liang Xia suddenly cried out: "But you haven't had your supper yet!" Mao Tou shook his head and left. Yuejun knew that his mother had died of a heart attack after a struggle meeting. Now he had no parents to look after him.

5

Despite disasters afflicting the society, time marched on. Tempered by grief, doubt and anxiety, the people came to see the truth.

On the eve of the Qing Ming Festival in April 1976, darkness enveloped Beijing's Tiananmen Square. But bright wreaths overlapped each other; the loyal hearts of the people challenged the sombre surroundings. Some wreaths were as high as a house, while others were very small. They stretched from the Martyrs' Monument to the avenue. It was like a great hall of mourning, unparalleled in history, made by the people for Premier Zhou. The pine trees, covered with white paper flowers of mourning, were like a bank of snow. Gaily decorated baskets hung from the lamp-posts. Balloons floated in the air with streamers inscribed with the words: "Premier Zhou Is Immortal!" The crowds in the square were like a vast moving sea. They were silent, though all were indignant and at the end of their patience. The flames of truth in their hearts at last were about to blaze.

If the truth could be seen, Yuejun thought, it was in that square. The people were prepared to give their lives for it. She knew Liang Xia came every day to copy down poems and see the wreaths. Yuejun and Liang Xia were making their way to the monument in the middle of the square. They hung their basket on a pine tree. It contained pure white flowers entwined with silver paper, which glistened like their tears.

Liang Xia remembered pacing in the quiet square in January after the premier's death when she heard people weeping. A middle-aged woman had lurched towards the monument crying: "Oh premier, what shall we do in future? What?..." Her cries were carried round the square and reverberated in Liang Xia's heart.

Suddenly Yuejun felt Liang Xia shudder. Looking

in the same direction, she saw a streamer by the monument which read: "Even if the monsters spew out poisonous flames, the people will vanquish them!" Though the street lights were dim, these words seemed ablaze. This was the strength of the people! The people had begun to fight back!

Yuejun and Liang Xia walked among the crowds who were engrossed in copying poems. Some far away couldn't see clearly, so others who were nearer to the monument read them aloud. If some had no paper, others would tear out pages from their notebooks. People wrote leaning on others' backs. All the crowds shared one purpose and cherished a deep love for Premier Zhou.

Unexpectedly Mao Tou appeared. With a serious expression, he whispered something in Liang Xia's ear. She hurriedly pulled Yuejun away from the crowd.

On their way home, Yuejun was filled with grief and anxiety. She wasn't afraid for herself, but very worried about Liang Xia and Mao Tou, and all the other young people in the square who were reciting poems. On reaching home, she sat down at the desk in front of a photograph of Premier Zhou, taken when he was young. Yuejun wished she could talk to Pei who had given her this photograph, but she had been in hospital because of a heart attack since March. She had been working too hard.

Liang Xia was busy on her "raft". After a moment she emerged and poured herself a glass of water. She looked calm and happy, though pale. "Would you like some water, auntie?" she asked. There was no answer.

Then Yuejun said looking at her: "I want to say

something to you. I guess you're going to put up some posters. It's too dangerous!" She paused before adding: "You're young. You must live to see the day. . . . You're the only survivor in your family."

Not in the least disturbed, Liang Xia replied: "I don't want to hide anything from you. But we must speak out and let those bastards know we are still living. As you know, I'm not afraid of anything."

Yuejun said after a pause, tears streaming down her face: "Then let me go! I'm old, but I can do it as well as you!"

"You?" Amazed, Liang Xia gazed at her kind, pleasant, tear-stained face. She too began to weep, though she tried to hold back her tears.

"Xia!" Yuejun hugged her tightly. Her tears dropped on the girl's hair, while Liang Xia's wet her breast.

Liang Xia soon dried her eyes. There was no time for a good cry. It was as if she heard the bugle call. Flames of love and hatred blazed in her heart, melting it. She had thought of telling Yuejun that she had already distributed some leaflets in the trolleys and parks. Some had expressed her views, while others contained only one sentence: "Down with the gang, the cause of all disasters!" She was sure there wouldn't be any trouble, but still it was better not to involve Yuejun. She decided to keep her in the dark and so she changed the subject: "All right, I won't go out now. Where are you going, auntie?"

"I'm serious, you little wretch!" Yuejun protested.

"So am I." She wiped away her tears. "You must rest. You're too excited." With this, she went to make up Yuejun's bed and quietly slipped two sleeping pills into a glass of water. Handing it to her, she persuaded Yuejun to lie down.

Soon Yuejun felt very sleepy so she lay down, while Liang Xia paced the floor, cheerfully. "You should put on something more," Yuejun advised, noticing Liang Xia was only wearing her woollen jersey. "You must take care of yourself!" Then she wondered if she was really getting old, as she was feeling so tired.

Yuejun fell asleep and was unaware that Liang Xia had tidied up the room. Before leaving, she had fondled the cello and turned to gaze again and again at the screen behind which was Yuejun's bed. Finally she made up her mind and gingerly opening the door went out. . . .

That night she didn't return. On the second and third nights she still hadn't come home.

One evening after her discharge from hospital, Pei came to visit Yuejun. It was already summer. Through the window the stars shone. The two women sat facing each other in silence. After a while, Yuejun took a notebook out of a drawer, saying: "I found this yesterday. Xia made notes in it."

Pei was startled when she flicked through the pages to read: "I won't live under the same sky with the sworn enemy of my family and my country!" She read the sentence again and again before saying confidently: "Don't be sad. I believe she'll come back one day."

Yuejun nodded: "I hope so. I know where Mao Tou is imprisoned. But I've no news about Xia."

"We'll try to locate her." The notebook was clenched tightly in Pei's hand.

Yuejun heaved a sigh: "Recently I feel as if we've

been playing a piece of music interminably but it may break off any moment now."

"Don't worry. We'll end this symphony on a magnificent, triumphant note. By the way, in the past two months, an instruction came from our ministry to investigate the relationship between you and Liang Xia, but we refused to do it."

Rising to her feet, Yuejun declared: "Tell them Liang Xia's my daughter. I'll adopt her as my own daughter." Her worn, sweet face brightened, and in her eyes shone determination.

Pei grasped her hand firmly.

That night Yuejun dreamed that she was playing her cello at a concert. The music from the cello was splendid and triumphant. In the audience a pair of dark eyes danced to the melody. They belonged to Liang Xia.

Then suddenly it was Liang Xia and not she who was playing on the stage. Her skilful playing was inspiring and encouraging. Happy tears poured down her cheeks. The stage lights shone on her white gauze and silver-threaded dress and on her glistening tears. The powerful music reverberated inside and outside the hall. She played what was in her heart and in the hearts of the people.

Translated by Song Shouquan

Shen Rong in 1980

Shen Rong

SHEN Rong, a native of Sichuan and daughter of a judge, was born in 1935 in Hankou. After the founding of New China she left junior middle school at the age of fifteen to be a salesgirl in a bookshop for workers. In '52 she transferred to the *Southwest Workers' Daily* in Chongqing, and in '54 she went to study Russian in Beijing. After graduation she worked as a translator in the Radio Station, then for reasons of health went to live with a peasant family in Shanxi. Back in Beijing in '64 she started writing plays. In the '70s she wrote several novels. "At Middle Age", published in 1980, won its author wider recognition, being generally admired for the skill and courage with which it raises the problems of middle-aged professionals, praising the heroes and heroines of our times and condemning those who hold up progress. Shen Rong is a member of the Chinese Writers' Association.

At Middle Age

Shen Rong

WERE the stars twinkling in the sky? Was a boat rocking on the sea? Lu Wenting, an oculist, lay on her back in hospital. Circles of light, bright or dim, appeared before her eyes. She seemed to be lifted by a cloud, up and down, drifting about without any direction.

Was she dreaming or dying?

She remembered vaguely going to the operating theatre that morning, putting on her operating gown and walking over to the wash-basin. Ah, yes, Jiang Yafen, her good friend, had volunteered to be her assistant. Having got their visas, Jiang and her family were soon leaving for Canada. This was their last operation as colleagues.

Together they washed their hands. They had been medical students in the same college in the fifties and, after graduation, had been assigned to the same hospital. As friends and colleagues for more than twenty years, they found it hard to part. This was no mood for a doctor to be in prior to an operation. Lu remembered she had wanted to say something to ease their sadness. What had she said? She had turned to Jiang and inquired, "Have you booked your plane tickets, Yafen?"

What had been her reply? She had said nothing, but her eyes had gone red. Then after a long time Jiang asked, "You think you can manage three operations in one morning?"

Lu couldn't remember what she had answered. She had probably gone on scrubbing her nails in silence. The new brush hurt her fingertips. She looked at the soap bubbles on her hands and glanced at the clock on the wall, strictly following the rules, brushing her hands, wrists and arms three times, three minutes each. Ten minutes later she soaked her arms in a pail of antiseptic, 75 per cent alcohol. It was white — maybe yellowish. Even now her hands and arms were numb and burning. From the alcohol? No. It was unlikely. They had never hurt before. Why couldn't she lift them?

She remembered that at the start of the operation, when she had injected novocaine behind the patient's eyeball, Yafen had asked softly, "Has your daughter got over her pneumonia?"

What was wrong with Jiang today? Didn't she know that when operating a surgeon should forget everything, including herself and her family, and concentrate on the patient? How could she inquire after Xiaojia at such a time? Perhaps, feeling miserable about leaving, she had forgotten that she was assisting at an operation.

A bit annoyed, Lu retorted, "I'm only thinking about this eye now."

She lowered her head and cut with a pair of curved scissors.

One operation after another. Why three in one morning? She had had to remove Vice-minister Jiao's cataract, transplant a cornea on Uncle Zhang's eye and correct Wang Xiaoman's squint. Starting at eight o'clock, she had sat on the high operating stool for four and a half hours, concentrating under a lamp. She had cut and stitched again and again. When she had finished the last one and put a piece of gauze on the patient's eye, she was stiff and her legs wouldn't move.

Having changed her clothes, Jiang called to her from the door, "Let's go, Wenting."

"You go first." She stayed where she was.

"I'll wait for you. It's my last time here." Jiang's eyes were watery. Was she crying? Why?

"Go on home and do your packing. Your husband must be waiting for you."

"He's already packed our things." Looking up, Jiang called, "What's wrong with your legs?"

"I've been sitting so long, they've gone to sleep! They'll be OK in a minute. I'll come to see you this evening."

"All right. See you then."

After Jiang had left, Lu moved back to the wall of white tiles, supporting herself with her hands against it for a long time before going to the changing-room.

She remembered putting on her grey jacket, leaving the hospital and reaching the lane leading to her home. All of a sudden she was exhausted, more tired than she had ever felt before. The lane became long and hazy, her home seemed far away. She felt she would never get there.

She became faint. She couldn't open her eyes, her lips felt dry and stiff. She was thirsty, very thirsty. Where could she get some water?

Her parched lips trembled.

2

"Look, Dr Sun, she's come to!" Jiang cried softly. She had been sitting beside Lu all the time.

Sun Yimin, head of the Ophthalmic Department, was reading Lu's case-history and was shocked by the diagnosis of myocardial infarction. Very worried, the greying man shook his head and pushed back his black-rimmed spectacles, recalling that Lu was not the first doctor aged about forty in his department who had fallen ill with heart disease. She had been a healthy woman of forty-two. This attack was too sudden and serious.

Sun turned his tall, stooping frame to look down at Lu's pale face. She was breathing weakly, her eyes closed, her dry lips trembling slightly.

"Dr Lu," Sun called softly.

She didn't move, her thin, puffy face expressionless.

"Wenting," Jiang urged.

Still no reaction.

Sun raised his eyes to the forbidding oxygen cylinder, which stood at a corner of the room and then looked at the ECG monitor. He was reassured when he saw a regular QRS wave on the oscillometer. He turned back to Lu, waved his hand and said, "Ask her husband to come in."

A good-looking, balding man in his forties, of medium height, entered quickly. He was Fu Jiajie, Lu's husband. He had spent a sleepless night beside her and had been reluctant to leave when Sun had sent him away to lie down on the bench outside the room.

As Sun made way for him, Fu bent down to look at the familiar face, which was now so pale and strange.

Lu's lips moved again. Nobody except her husband understood her. He said, "She wants some water. She's thirsty."

Jiang gave him a small teapot. Carefully, Fu avoided the rubber tube leading from the oxygen cylinder and put it to Lu's parched lips. Drop by drop, the water trickled into the dying woman's mouth.

"Wenting, Wenting," Fu called.

When a drop of water fell from Fu's shaking hand on to Lu's pallid face, the muscles seemed to twitch a little.

3

Eyes. Eyes. Eyes....

Many flashed past Lu's closed ones. Eyes of men and women, old and young, big and small, bright and dull, all kinds, blinking at her.

Ah! These were her husband's eyes. In them, she saw joy and sorrow, anxiety and pleasure, suffering and hope. She could see through his eyes, his heart. His eyes were as bright as the golden sun in the sky. His loving heart had given her so much warmth. It was his voice, Jiajie's voice, so endearing, so gentle, and so far away, as if from another world:

> "I wish I were a rapid stream,
> ......
> If my love
> A tiny fish would be,
> She'd frolic
> In my foaming waves."

Where was she? Oh, she was in a park covered with snow. There was a frozen lake, clear as crystal, on which red, blue, purple and white figures skated. Happy laughter resounded in the air while they moved arm in arm, threading their way through the crowds. She saw none of the smiling faces around her, only his. They slid on the ice, side by side, twirling, laughing. What bliss!

The ancient Five Dragon Pavilions shrouded in snow were solemn, tranquil and deserted. They leaned against the white marble balustrades, while snowflakes covered them. Holding hands tightly, they defied the severe cold.

She was young then.

She had never expected love or special happiness. Her father had deserted her mother when she was a girl, and her mother had had a hard time raising her alone. Her childhood had been bleak. All she remembered was a mother prematurely old who, night after night, sewed under a solitary lamp.

She boarded at her medical college, rising before daybreak to memorize new English words, going to classes and filling scores of notebooks with neat little characters. In the evenings she studied in the library and then worked late into the night doing autopsies. She never grudged spending her youth studying.

Love had no place in her life. She shared a room with Jiang Yafen, her classmate, who had beautiful eyes, bewitching lips and who was tall, slim and lively. Every week, Jiang received love letters. Every weekend, she dated, while poor Lu did nothing, neglected by everyone.

After graduation, she and Jiang were assigned to the

same hospital, which had been founded more than a hundred years earlier. Their internship lasted for four years, during which time they had to be in the hospital all day long, and remain single.

Secretly, Jiang cursed these rules, while Lu accepted the terms willingly. What did it matter being in the hospital twenty-four hours a day? She would have liked to be there forty-eight hours, if possible. No marriage for four years. Hadn't many skilled doctors married late or remained single all their lives? So she threw herself heart and soul into her work.

But life is strange. Fu Jiajie suddenly entered her quiet, routine life.

She never understood how it happened. He had been hospitalized because of an eye disease. She was his doctor. Perhaps, his feelings for her arose from her conscientious treatment. Passionate and deep, his emotions changed both their lives.

Winter in the north is always very cold, but that winter he gave her warmth. Never having imagined love could be so intoxicating, she almost regretted not finding it earlier. She was already twenty-eight, yet she still had the heart of a young girl. With her whole being, she welcomed this late love.

> "I wish I were a deserted forest,
> . . . . . .
> If my love
> A little bird would be,
> She'd nest and twitter
> In my dense trees."

Incredible that Fu Jiajie, whom Jiang regarded as a bookworm and who was doing research on a new material for a spacecraft in the Metallurgical Research Institute, could read poetry so well!

"Who wrote it?" Lu asked.

"The Hungarian poet Petöfi."

"Does a scientist have time for poetry?"

"A scientist must have imagination. Science has something in common with poetry in this respect."

Pedantic? He gave good answers.

"What about you? Do you like poetry?" he asked.

"Me? I don't know anything about it. I seldom read it." She smiled cynically. "The Ophthalmic Department does operations. Every stitch, every incision is strictly laid down. We can't use the slightest imagination. . . ."

Fu cut in, "Your work is a beautiful poem. You can make many people see again. . . ."

Smiling, he moved over to her, his face close to hers. His masculinity, which she had never experienced before, assailed, bewildered and unnerved her. She felt something must happen, and, sure enough, he put his arms round her, embracing her tightly.

It had occurred so suddenly that she looked fearfully at the smiling eyes close to hers and his parted lips. Her heart thumping, her head raised, she closed her eyes in embarrassment, moving away instinctively as his irresistible love flooded her.

Beihai Park in the snow was just the right place for her. Snow covered the tall dagoba, Qiongdao Islet with its green pines, the long corridor and quiet lake. It also hid the sweet shyness of the lovers.

To everyone's surprise, after her four-year internship had ended, Lu was the first to get married. Fate had decided Fu Jiajie's intrusion. How could she refuse

his wish that they marry? How insistently and strongly
he wanted her, preparing to sacrifice everything for her!
· · ·

"I wish I were a crumbling ruin,
· · · · · ·
If my love
Green ivy would be,
She'd tenderly entwine
Around my lonely head."

Life was good, love was beautiful. These recollec-
tions gave her strength, and her eyelids opened slightly.

4

After heavy dosages of sedatives and analgesics Dr
Lu was still in a coma. The head of the Internal
Medicine Department gave her a careful examination,
studied her ECG and her case-history, then told the
ward doctor to keep up the intravenous drip and injections of opiate and morphine and to watch out for
changes in her ECG monitor to guard against more
serious complications due to myocardial infarction.

On leaving the ward he remarked to Sun, "She's
too weak. I remember how fit Dr Lu was when she
first came here."

"Yes." Sun shook his head with a sigh. "It's
eighteen years since she came to our hospital, just a
girl."

Eighteen years ago Dr Sun had already been a well-
known ophthalmologist, respected by all his colleagues
for his skill and responsible attitude to work. This

able, energetic professor in his prime regarded it as his duty to train the younger doctors. Each time the medical college assigned them a new batch of graduates, he examined them one by one to make his choice. He thought the first step to making their Ophthalmology Department the best in all China was by selecting the most promising interns.

How had he chosen Lu? He remembered quite distinctly. At first this twenty-four-year-old graduate had not made much of an impression on him.

That morning Department Head Sun had already interviewed five of the graduates assigned to them and had been most disappointed. Some of them were suitable, but they were not interested in the Ophthalmology Department and did not want to work there. Others wanted to be oculists because they thought it a simple, easy job. By the time he picked up the sixth file marked Lu Wenting, he was rather tired and not expecting much. He was reflecting that the medical college's teaching needed improving to give students a correct impression from the start of his department.

The door opened quietly. A slim girl walked softly in. Looking up he saw that she had on a cotton jacket and slacks. Her cuffs were patched, the knees of her blue slacks were faded. Simply dressed, she was even rather shabby. He read the name on her file, then glanced at her casually. She really looked like a little girl, slightly built, with an oval face and neatly bobbed glossy black hair. She calmly sat down on the chair facing him.

Asked the usual technical questions, she answered each in turn, saying no more than was strictly necessary.

"You want to work in the Ophthalmology Department?" Sun asked lethargically, having almost decided to wind up this interview. His elbows on the desk, he rubbed his temples with his fingers.

"Yes. At college I was interested in ophthalmology." She spoke with a slight southern accent.

Delighted by this answer, Sun lowered his hands as if his head no longer ached. He had changed his mind. Watching her carefully he asked more seriously, "What aroused your interest?"

At once this question struck him as inappropriate, too hard to answer. But she replied confidently, "Ophathalmology is lagging behind in our country."

"Good, tell me in what way it's backward," he asked eagerly.

"I don't know how to put it, but I feel we haven't tried out certain operations which are done abroad. Such as using laser beams to seal retina wounds. I think we ought to try these methods too."

"Right!" Mentally, Sun had already given her full marks. "What else? Any other ideas?"

"Yes ... well ... making more use of freezing to remove cataracts. Anyway, it seems to me there are many new problems that ought to be studied."

"Good, that makes sense. Can you read foreign materials?"

"With difficulty, using a dictionary. I like foreign languages."

"Excellent."

That was the first time Sun had praised a new student like this to her face. A few days later Lu Wenting and Jiang Yafen were the first to be admitted to his department. Sun chose Jiang for her intelligence, enthusiasm and enterprise, Lu for her simplicity, seriousness and keenness.

The first year they performed external ocular operations and studied ophthalmology. The second year they operated on eyeballs and studied ophthalmometry and ophthalmomyology. By the third year they were able to do such tricky operations as on cataract cases. That year something happened which made Sun see Lu in a new light.

It was a spring morning, a Monday. Sun made his round of the wards followed by white-coated doctors, some senior, some junior. The patients were sitting up in bed expectantly, hoping this famous professor would examine their eyes, as if with one touch of his hand he could heal them.

Each time he came to a bed, Sun picked up the case-history hanging behind it and read it while listening to the attending oculist or some senior oculist report on the diagnosis and treatment. Sometimes he raised a patient's eyelid to look at his eye, sometimes patted him on the shoulder and urged him not to worry about his operation, then moved on to the next bed.

After the ward round they held a short consultation, at which tasks were assigned. It was generally Dr Sun and the attending oculists who spoke, while the residents listened carefully, not venturing to speak for fear of making fools of themselves in front of these authorities. Today was the same. All that had to be said had been said and tasks were assigned. As he stood up to leave, Sun asked, "Have the rest of you anything to add?"

A girl spoke up in a low voice from one corner of the room, "Dr Sun, will you please have another look at the photograph of the patient in Bed 3 Ward 4?"

All heads turned in her direction. Sun saw that the speaker was Lu. She was so short, so inconspicuous, that he had not noticed her following him in the wards. Back in the office where they had talked at some length, he had still not noticed her presence.

"Bed 3?" He turned to the chief resident.

"An industrial accident," he was told.

"When he was admitted to hospital a picture was taken of his eye," Lu said. "The radiologists' report said there was no sign of a metal foreign body. After hospitalization the wound was sewn up and healed, but the patient complained of pain. I had another X-ray taken, and I believe there really is a foreign body. Will you have a look, Dr Sun?"

The film was fetched. Sun examined it. The chief resident and attending oculists then passed it round.

Jiang looked wide-eyed at her classmate, thinking, "Couldn't you have waited until after the meeting to ask Dr Sun to look at that? If by any chance you're wrong, the whole department will gossip. Even if you're right, you're implying that the doctors in the Outpatients Department are careless, and they are attending oculists!"

"You're right, there's a foreign body." Sun took back the picture and nodded. Looking round at the others he said, "Dr Lu has not been long in our department. Her careful, responsible attitude is admirable, and so is her hard study."

Lu lowered her head. This unexpected praise in public made her blush. At sight of this Sun smiled. He knew it took great courage and a strong sense of responsibility for a resident oculist to challenge an attending one's diagnosis.

Hospitals have a more complex hierarchy than other organizations. It was an unwritten rule that junior doctors should defer to their seniors; residents should obey the attending doctors; and there could be no disputing the opinions of professors and associate professors. So Sun attached special importance to Lu's query, since she was so very junior.

From then on his estimate of Lu was, "She's a very promising oculist."

Now eighteen years had passed. Lu, Jiang and their age group had become the backbone of his department. If promotion had been based on competence, they should long ago have had the rank of department heads. But this had not happened, and they were still not even attending doctors. For eighteen years their status had been that of interns, for the "cultural revolution" had broken the ladder leading to promotion.

The sight of Lu at her last gasp filled him with compassion. He stopped the head of the Internal Medicine Department to ask, "What do you think? Will she pull through?"

The department head looked towards her ward and sighed, then shook his head and said softly, "Old Sun, we can only hope she'll soon be out of danger."

Sun walked back anxiously to the ward. His steps were heavy, he was showing his age. From the doorway he saw Jiang still beside Lu's pillow. He halted, not wanting to disturb the two close friends.

In late autumn the nights are long. Darkness fell before six. The soughing wind rustled the phoenix trees outside the window. One by one their withered yellow leaves were blown away.

Sun, watching the whirling yellow leaves outside and

listening to the wind, felt gloomier than before. Of these two skilled ophthamologists, two key members of his staff, one had collapsed and might never recover, the other was leaving and might never return. They were two of the mainstays of his department in this prestigious hospital. Without them, he felt his department would be like the phoenix trees buffeted by the wind. It would deteriorate from day to day.

5

She seemed to be walking along an endless road, not a winding mountain path which urged people on, nor a narrow one between fields of fragrant rice. This was a desert, a quagmire, a wasteland, devoid of people and silent. Walking was difficult and exhausting.

Lie down and rest. The desert was warm, the quagmire soft. Let the ground warm her rigid body, the sunshine caress her tired limbs. Death was calling softly, "Rest, Dr Lu!"

Lie down and rest. Everlasting rest. No thoughts, feelings, worries, sadness or exhaustion.

But she couldn't do that. At the end of the long road, her patients were waiting for her. She seemed to see one patient tossing and turning in bed with the pain in his eyes, crying quietly at the threat of blindness. She saw many eager eyes waiting for her. She heard her patients calling to her in despair, "Dr Lu!"

This was a sacred call, an irresistible one. She trudged on the long road dragging her numb legs, from her home to the hospital, from the clinic to the ward, from one village to another with a medical team. Day by day, month by month, year by year, she trudged on. . . .

"Dr Lu!"

Who was calling? Director Zhao? Yes. He had called her by phone. She remembered putting down the receiver, handing over her patient to Jiang, who shared her consulting room, and heading for the director's office.

She hurried through a small garden, ignoring the white and yellow chrysanthemums, the fragrance of the osmanthus and the fluttering butterflies. She wanted to quickly finish her business with Zhao and return to her patients. There were seventeen waiting that morning, and she had only seen seven so far. Tomorrow she was on ward duty. She wanted to make arrangements for some of the out-patients.

She remembered not knocking but walking straight in. A man and woman were sitting on the sofa. Sha halted. Then she saw Director Zhao in his swivel-chair.

"Come in please, Dr Lu," Zhao greeted her.

She walked over and sat down on a leather chair by the window.

The large room was bright, tidy and quiet, unlike the noisy clinic, where sometimes the children howled. She felt odd, unused to the quietness and cleanliness of the room.

The couple looked cultured and composed. Director Zhao was always erect and scholarly looking, with well-groomed hair, a kind face and smiling eyes behind gold-rimmed spectacles. He had on a white shirt, a well-pressed light grey suit and shining black leather shoes.

The man sitting on the sofa was tall and greying at the temples. A pair of sun-glasses shielded his eyes. Lu saw at a glance that he had eye trouble. Leaning back against the sofa, he was playing with his walking-stick.

The woman in her fifties was still attractive, despite her age. Though her hair was dyed and permed, it did not look cheap. Her clothes were well-cut and expensive.

Lu remembered how the woman had sized her up, following her about with her eyes. Her face showed doubt, uneasiness and disappointment.

"Dr Lu, let me introduce you to Vice-minister Jiao Chengsi and his wife Comrade Qin Bo."

A vice-minister? Well, in the past ten years and more, she had treated many ministers, Party secretaries and directors. She had never paid attention to titles. She simply wondered what was wrong with his eyes. Was he losing his sight?

Director Zhao asked, "Dr Lu, are you in the clinic or on duty in the ward?"

"Starting from tomorrow, I'll be on ward duty."

"Fine," he laughed. "Vice-minister Jiao wants to have his cataract removed."

That meant she was given the task. She asked the man, "Is it one eye?"

"Yes."

"Which one?"

"The left one."

"Can't you see with it at all?"

The patient shook his head.

"Did you see a doctor before?"

As she rose to examine his eye, she remembered he named a hospital. Then his wife, who was sitting beside him, politely stopped her.

"There's no hurry, Dr Lu. Sit down, please. We

ought to go to your clinic for an examination." Smiling, Qin Bo turned to Director Zhao. "Since he developed eye trouble, I've become something of an oculist myself."

Though Lu didn't examine him, she stayed a long time. What had they talked about? Qin had asked her many personal questions.

"How long have you been here, Dr Lu?"

She hadn't kept track of the years. She only remembered the year she had graduated. So she answered, "I came here in 1961."

"Eighteen years ago." Qin counted on her fingers.

Why was she so interested in this? Then Director Zhao chipped in, "Dr Lu has a lot of experience. She's a skilled surgeon."

Qin went on, "You don't seem to be in good health, Dr Lu."

What was she driving at? Lu was so busy caring for others, that she had never given any thought to her own health. The hospital didn't even have her case-history. And none of her leaders had ever inquired after her health. Why was this stranger showing such concern? She hesitated before answering, "I'm very well."

Zhao added again, "She's one of the fittest. Dr Lu's never missed a day's work for years."

Lu made no answer, wondering why this was so important to this lady, and fretting to get back to her patients. Jiang couldn't possibly cope with so many alone.

Her eyes fixed on Lu, the lady smiled and pressed, "Are you sure you can remove a cataract easily, Dr Lu?"

Another difficult question. She had had no accidents

so far, but anything could happen if the patient didn't co-operate well or if the anaesthetic was not carefully applied.

She couldn't recollect whether she had made a reply, only Qin's big eyes staring at her with doubt, unsettling her. Having treated all kinds of patients, she had got used to the difficult wives of high cadres. She was searching for a tactful answer when Jiao moved impatiently and turned his head to his wife, who stopped and averted her gaze.

How had this trying conversation finished? Oh, yes, Jiang had come to tell her that Uncle Zhang had come for his appointment.

Qin quickly said politely, "You can go, Dr Lu, if you're busy."

Lu left the big bright room, which was so suffocating. She could hardly breathe.

She was suffocating.

6

Shortly before the day ended, Director Zhao hurried over to the internal medicine ward.

"Dr Lu's always enjoyed good health, Dr Sun. Why should she have this sudden attack?" his hands in his pockets, Zhao asked Sun as they headed for Lu's ward. Eight years Sun's junior, Zhao looked much younger, his voice more powerful.

He shook his head and went on, "This is a warning. Middle-aged doctors are the backbone of our hospital. Their heavy responsibilities and daily chores are ruining their health. If they collapse one by one, we'll be in a fix. How many people are there in her family? How many rooms does she have?"

Looking at Sun, who was depressed and worried, he added, "What? . . . Four in a room? So that's how it is! What's her wage? . . . 56.50 yuan! That's why people say better to be a barber with a razor than a surgeon with a scalpel. There's some truth in it. Right? Why wasn't her salary raised last year?"

"There were too many. You can't raise everyone's," Sun said cynically.

"I hope you'll talk that problem over with the Party branch. Ask them to investigate the work, income and living conditions of the middle-aged doctors and send me a report."

"What's the use of that? A similar report was sent in in 1978," Sun retorted politely, his eyes on the ground.

"Stop grumbling, Dr Sun. A report's better than nothing. I can show it to the municipal Party committee, the Ministry of Health and whomever it concerns. The Central Party Committee has stressed time and again that talented people and intellectuals should be valued and their salaries increased. We can't ignore it. The day before yesterday, at a meeting of the municipal committee, it was stressed that atttention should be paid to middle-aged personnel. I believe their problems will be solved." Zhao stopped when they entered Lu's room.

Fu Jiajie stood up as Zhao entered. He waved his hand in greeting and walked over to Lu, bent down and examined her face. Then he took her case-history from her doctor. From a director he had turned into a doctor.

Zhao, a noted thorax expert, had returned to China after Liberation. Very enthusiastic politically, he was praised for both his political consciousness and his medical skill, joining the Party in the fifties. When later he was made director, he had to take part in so many meetings and do so much administrative work, that he seldom found the opportunity to see patients except for important consultations. During the "cultural revolution", he had been detained illegally and made to sweep the hospital grounds. The last three years, as director again, he had been so tied up with daily problems that he practically had no time or energy for surgery.

Now he had come specially to see Lu. All the ward doctors had gathered behind him.

But he didn't say anything startling. Having read the case-history and looked at the ECG monitor, he told the doctors to note any changes and watch out for complications. Then he asked, "Is her husband here?"

Sun introduced Fu. Zhao wondered why this charming man in his prime was already going bald. Apparently, a man who didn't know how to look after himself couldn't look after his wife either.

"It won't be easy," Zhao told him. "She needs complete rest. She'll need help for everything, even to turn over in bed. Help twenty-four hours a day. Where do you work? You'll have to ask for leave. You can't do it all by yourself either. Is there anyone else in your family?"

Fu shook his head. "Just two small children."

Zhao turned to Sun, "Can you spare someone from your department?"

"For one or two days, maybe."

"That'll do to begin with."

His eyes returning to Lu's thin pale face, Zhao still couldn't understand why this energetic woman had suddenly collapsed.

It occurred to him that she might have been too nervous operating on Vice-minister Jiao. Then he dismissed the thought. She was experienced and it was highly improbable that an attack had been brought on by nervousness. Besides, myocardial infarction often had no obvious cause.

But he couldn't dismiss the notion that there was some kind of a link between Jiao's operation and Lu's illness. He regretted having recommended her. In fact, Jiao's wife, Qin Bo, had been reluctant to have her right from the beginning.

That day, after Lu's departure, Qin had asked, "Director Zhao, is Dr Lu the vice-head of her department?"

"No."

"Is she an attending doctor?"

"No."

"Is she a Party member?"

"No."

Qin said bluntly, "Excuse my outspokenness since we're all Party members, but I think it's rather inappropriate to let an ordinary doctor operate on Vice-minister Jiao."

Jiao stopped her by banging his walking-stick on the floor. Turning to her he said angrily, "What are you talking about, Qin Bo? Let the hospital make the arrangements. Any surgeon can operate."

Qin retorted heatedly, "That's not the right attitude, Old Jiao. You must be responsible. You can work only if you're healthy. We must be responsible to the revolution and the Party."

Zhao quickly butted in to avoid a quarrel, "Believe me, Comrade Qin, although she's not a Communist, Lu's a good doctor. And she's very good at removing cataracts. Don't worry!"

"It's not that, Director Zhao. And I'm not being too careful either." Qin sighed, "When I was in the cadre school, one old comrade had to have that operation. He was not allowed to come back to Beijing. So he went to a small hospital there. Before the operation was through his eyeball fell out. Jiao was detained by the followers of the gang for seven years! He has just resumed work. He can't do without his eyes."

"Nothing like that will happen, Comrade Qin. We've very few accidents in our hospital."

Qin still tried to argue her point. "Can we ask Dr Sun, the department head, to operate on Jiao?"

Zhao shook his head and laughed. "Dr Sun's almost seventy and has poor eyesight himself! Besides, he hasn't operated for years. He does research, advises the younger doctors and teaches. Dr Lu's a better surgeon than he."

"How about Dr Guo then?"

Zhao stared. "Dr Guo?" She must have made a thorough investigation of the department.

She prompted, "Guo Ruqing."

Zhao gestured helplessly. "He's left the country."

Qin wouldn't give up. "When is he coming back?"

"He's not."

"What do you mean?" This time she stared.

Zhao sighed. "Dr Guo's wife returned from abroad. When her father, a shopkeeper, died, he left his store to them. So they decided to leave."

"To leave medicine for a store? I can't understand it." Jiao sighed too.

"He's not the only one. Several of our capable doctors have left or are preparing to go."

Qin was indignant. "I don't understand their mentality."

Jiao waved his stick and turned to Zhao, "In the early fifties, intellectuals like you overcame many difficulties to return here to help build a new China. But now, the intellectuals we've trained are leaving the country. It's a serious lesson."

"This can't go on," said Qin. "We must do more ideological work. After the gang was smashed, the social status of intellectuals was raised a lot. Their living and working conditions will improve as China modernizes."

"Yes. Our Party committee holds the same view. I talked with Dr Guo twice on behalf of the Party and begged him to stay. But it was no use."

Qin, who was about to continue, was stopped by Jiao who said, "Director Zhao, I didn't come to insist on having an expert or a professor. I came because I've confidence in your hospital, or to be exact, because I have a special feeling for your hospital. A few years ago, the cataract in my right eye was removed here. And it was superbly done."

"Who did it?" Zhao asked.

Jiao answered sadly, "I never found out who she was."

"That's easy. We can look up your case-history."

Zhao picked up the receiver, thinking that Qin would be satisfied if he got that doctor. But Jiao stopped him. "You can't find her. I had it done as an out-patient. There was no case-history. It was a woman with a southern accent."

"That's difficult." Zhao laughed, replacing the receiver. "We have many women doctors who speak with a southern accent. Dr Lu also comes from the south. Let her do it."

The couple agreed. Qin helped Jiao up and they left.

Was this the cause of Lu's illness? Zhao couldn't believe it. She had performed this operation hundreds of times. She wouldn't be so nervous. He had gone over before the operation and found her confident, composed and well. Why this sudden attack, then?

Zhao looked again at Lu with concern. Even on the brink of death, she looked as if she were sleeping peacefully.

7

Lu was always composed, quiet and never flustered. Another woman would have retorted or shown her indignation at Qin's insulting questions or, at very least, felt resentful afterwards. But Lu had left Zhao's office as calm as ever, neither honoured to be chosen to operate on Vice-minister Jiao nor humiliated by Qin's questions. The patient had the right to decide whether or not he wanted an operation. That was all there was to it.

"Well, what big official wants you this time?" Jiang asked softly.

"It's not definite yet."

"Let's hurry." Jiang steered her along. "I couldn't persuade your Uncle Zhang. He's made up his mind not to have the operation."

"That's nonsense! He's travelled a long way to get

here and spent much money. He'll be able to see after the transplant. It's our duty to cure him."

"Then you talk him round."

Passing by the waiting-room, they smiled and nodded at the familiar patients who stood up to greet them. Back in her room, while Lu was seeing a young man, she was interrupted by a voice booming, "Dr Lu!"

Both Lu and her patient looked up as a tall sturdy man advanced. In his fifties, he was broad-shouldered, wearing black trousers and a shirt and a white towel round his head. At his cry, the people in the corridor quickly made way for him. A head above everyone else and almost blind, he was unaware that he attracted so much attention as he groped his way in the direction of Lu's voice.

Lu hurried forward to help him. "Sit down, please, Uncle Zhang."

"Thank you, Dr Lu. I want to tell you something."

"Yes, but sit down first." Lu helped him to a chair.

"I've been in Beijing quite a while now. I'm thinking of going home tomorrow and coming back some other time."

"I don't agree. You've come such a long way and spent so much money...."

"That's just it," Uncle Zhang cut in, slapping his thigh. "So I think I'll go home, do some work and earn some more workpoints. Although I can't see, I can still do some work and the brigade's very kind to me. I've made up my mind to leave, Dr Lu. But I couldn't go without saying goodbye to you. You've done so much for me."

Having suffered from corneal ulcers for many years, he had come to the hospital to have a transplant, a suggestion proposed by Lu when she had visited his brigade with a medical team.

"Your son spent a lot of money to send you here. We can't let you go home like this."

"I feel better already!"

Lu laughed. "When you're cured, you can work for another twenty years since you're so strong."

Uncle Zhang laughed. "You bet I will! I can do anything if my eyes are good."

"Then stay and have them treated."

Zhang confided, "Listen, Dr Lu, I'll tell you the truth. I'm worried about money. I can't afford to live in a Beijing hotel."

Stunned, Lu quickly told him, "I know you're next on the list. Once there's a donor, it'll be your turn."

He finally agreed to stay. Lu helped him out. Then a little girl of eleven accosted her.

Her pretty, rosy face was marred by a squint. Dressed in hospital pyjamas, she called timidly, "Dr Lu."

"Why don't you stay in the ward, Wang Xiaoman?" She had been admitted the previous day.

"I'm scared. I want to go home." She began to cry. "I don't want an operation."

Lu put one arm around her. "Tell me why you don't want an operation."

"It'll hurt too much."

"It won't, you silly girl! I'll give you an anaesthetic. It won't hurt at all." Lu patted her head and bent down to look with regret at the damaged work of art. She said, "Look, won't it be nice when I make this eye look like the other one? Now go back to your ward. You mustn't run around in a hospital."

When the little girl had wiped away her tears and left, Lu returned to her patients.

There had been many patients the last few days. She must make up for the time she had lost in Zhao's office. Forgetting Jiao, Qin and herself, she saw one patient after another.

A nurse came to tell her she was wanted on the phone.

Lu excused herself.

It was the kindergarten nurse informing her, "Xiao-jia has a temperature. It started last night. I know you're busy, so I took her to the doctor, who gave her an injection. She's still feverish and is asking for you. Can you come?"

"I'll be there in a minute." She replaced the receiver.

But she couldn't go immediately since many patients were waiting. She rang her husband, but was told that he had gone out to a meeting.

Back in her office, Jiang asked, "Who called? Anything important?"

"Nothing."

Lu never troubled others, not even her leaders. "I'll go to the kindergarten when I'm through with the patients," she thought as she returned to her desk. At first she imagined her daughter crying and calling her. Later she saw only the patients' eyes. She hurried to the kindergarten when she had finished.

8

"Why did it take you so long?" the nurse complained.

Lu walked quickly to the isolation room where her

little daughter lay, her face flushed with fever, her lips parted, her eyes closed, her breathing difficult.

She bent over the crib. "Mummy's here, darling."

Xiaojia moved and called in a hoarse voice, "Mummy, let's go home."

"All right, my pet."

She first took Xiaojia to her own hospital to see a pediatrician. "It's pneumonia," the sympathetic doctor told her. "You must take good care of her."

She nodded and left after Xiaojia had been given an injection and some medicine.

In the hospital everything stood still at noon, the outpatients having left, the in-patients sleeping and the hospital staff resting. The spacious grounds were deserted except for the chirping sparrows flying among the trees. Nature still competed with men in this noisy centre of the city, where tall buildings rose compactly and the air was polluted. In the hospital all day, Lu had never been aware of the birds before.

She couldn't make up her mind where to take her daughter, hating to leave the sick child alone in the kindergarten's isolation room. But who could look after her at home?

After some hesitation she steeled herself and headed for the kindergarten.

"No. I don't want to go there," Xiaojia wailed on her shoulder.

"Be a good girl, Xiaojia. . . ."

"No. I want to go home!" She began kicking.

"All right. We'll go home."

They had to go along a busy street with recently pasted advertisements of the latest fashions. Lu never so much as glanced at the costly goods in the shop-windows, or the produce the peasants sold in the streets. With two children, it was hard to make ends meet. Now, carrying Xiaojia in her arms and worrying about Yuanyuan at home, she was even less eager to look around.

Arriving home at one o'clock, Lu found a pouting Yuanyuan waiting for her. "Why are you so late, mummy?" he asked.

"Xiaojia's ill," Lu answered curtly, putting Xiaojia on the bed, undressing her and tucking her in.

Standing at the table Yuanyuan fretted, "Please cook lunch, mummy. I'll be late."

In frustration, Lu shouted at him, "You'll drive me crazy if you go on like that!"

Wronged and in a hurry, Yuanyuan was on the point of tears. Ignoring him, Lu went to stoke up the fire, which had almost gone out. The pots and the cupboard were empty. There were no left-overs from yesterday's meals.

She went back into the room, reproaching herself for having been so harsh on the poor boy.

In the past few years, keeping house had become an increasing burden. During the "cultural revolution" her husband's laboratory had been closed down and his research project scrapped. All he had needed to do was to show his face in the office for an hour in the morning and afternoon. He spent the remainder of his day and talents on domestic chores, cooking and learning to sew and knit, lifting the burden entirely from Lu's shoulders. After the gang was smashed, scientific research was resumed and Fu, a capable metallurgist, was busy again. Most of the housework was shouldered once more by Lu.

Every day at noon, she went home to cook. It was an effort to stoke up the fire, prepare the vegetables and be ready to serve the meal in fifty minutes so that Yuanyuan, Fu and herself could return to school or work on time.

When anything unexpected cropped up, the whole family went hungry. She sighed and gave her son some money. "Go and buy yourself a bun, Yuanyuan."

He turned back half-way, "What about you, mummy?"

"I'm not hungry."

"I'll buy you a bun too."

Yuanyuan soon came home with two buns and gave one to his mother. He left for school immediately, eating his on the way.

Biting into the cold hard bun, Lu looked around at her small room, which was twelve metres square.

She and her husband had been content with a simple life, living in this room since their marriage, without a sofa, wardrobe or a new desk. They had the same furniture they had used when they were single.

Though they owned few material possessions, they had many books. Aunt Chen, a neighbour, had commented, "What will the two bookworms live on?" But they were happy. All they had wanted was a small room, some clothes, and three simple meals a day.

Treasuring their time, they put their evenings to good use. Every night, when their neighbours' naughty children peeped into their small room to spy on the new couple, they invariably found them at work: Lu occupying their only desk studying foreign material with the help of a dictionary and taking notes, while Fu read reference books on a stack of chests.

The evening was not wasted when they could study late quietly and undisturbed. In the summer, their neighbours sat cooling themselves in the courtyard, but the smell of tea, the light breeze, bright stars, interesting news and conversation . . . none of these could lure them from their stuffy little room.

Their quiet life and studious evenings ended much too soon. Lu gave birth to Yuanyuan and then to Xiaojia. Their lovely children brought disorder and hardship as well as joy to their lives. When the crib was later replaced by a single bed and the tiny room filled with children's clothes, pots and pans, they could hardly move about. Peace was shattered by their children laughing and crying.

What could an oculist achieve without keeping up with foreign developments in the field? Therefore, Lu often sat reading behind a curtain in the room late into the night.

When Yuanyuan began school he had to use their only desk. Only when he had finished doing his homework was it Lu's turn to spread out her notebook and the medical books she had borrowed. Fu came last.

How hard life was!

Lu fixed her eyes on the little clock: One five, one ten, one fifteen. Time to go to work. What should she do? Lots of things needed winding up before she went to the ward tomorrow. What about Xiaojia? Should she call her husband? There was no telephone booth near by and, anyway, she probably could not get him. As he had wasted ten years, better not disturb him.

She frowned, at a loss what to do.

Perhaps she shouldn't have married. Some claimed that marriage ended love. She had naively believed that, though it might be true for some, it could not happen to her. If she had been more prudent, she would not have been weighed down by the burdens of marriage and a family.

One twenty. She must turn to her neighbour Aunt Chen, a kind-hearted woman who had helped on many occasions.... Since she would not accept anything for her services, Lu was reluctant to trouble her.

Still she had to this time. Aunt Chen was most obliging, "Leave her to me, Dr Lu."

Lu put some children's books and building blocks beside Xiaojia, asked Aunt Chen to give her the medicine and hurried to the hospital.

She had intended to tell the nurse not to send her too many patients so that she could go home early, but once she started work, she forgot everything.

Zhao called her up to remind her that Jiao was to be admitted the following day.

Qin called twice asking about the operation and how Jiao and his family should prepare mentally and materially.

Lu was hard put to it to give an answer. She had performed hundreds of such operations and no one had ever asked her that before. So she said, "Oh, nothing special."

"Really? But surely it's better to be well prepared. What if I come over and we have a chat?"

Lu quickly told her, "I'm busy this afternoon."

"Then we'll talk tomorrow in the hospital."

"OK."

When the trying conversation had ended, Lu had returned to her office. It was dark before she had finished her clinic.

Arriving home she heard Aunt Chen singing an impromptu song:

"Grow up, my dear,
    To be an engineer."

Xiaojia laughed happily. Lu thanked Aunt Chen and was relieved to find Xiaojia's temperature down.

She gave her an injection. After Fu returned, Jiang Yafen and her husband, Liu, called.

"We've come to say goodbye," said Jiang.

"Where are you going?" Lu inquired.

"We've just got our visas for Canada," replied Jiang, her eyes fixed on the ground.

Liu's father, a doctor in Canada, had urged them to join him there. Lu had not expected them to go.

"How long will you stay? When will you come back?" she asked.

"Maybe for good." Liu shrugged his shoulders.

"Why didn't you let me know earlier, Yafen?" Lu turned to her friend.

"I was afraid that you'd try to stop me. I was afraid I'd change my mind." Jiang avoided her eyes, staring hard at the ground.

From his bag, Liu produced some wine and food and said in high spirits, "I bet you haven't cooked yet. Let's have our farewell banquet here."

9

It was a sorrowful farewell party that evening.

They seemed to be drinking tears instead of wine. To be tasting the bitterness of life instead of delicious dishes,

Xiaojia was asleep, Yuanyuan watching TV next door. Liu raised his cup, eyeing the wine in it, and said with feeling, "Life — it's hard to tell how life will turn out! My father was a doctor with a sound classical education. As a child I loved old poetry and longed to become a writer, but I was fated to follow in his footsteps, and now over thirty years have gone. My father was extremely circumspect. His maxim was 'Too much talk leads to trouble'. Unfortunately I didn't take after him. I like talking and airing my views, so that landed me in trouble and I got bashed in each political movement. When graduated in '57, by the skin of my teeth I missed being labelled a Rightist. In the 'cultural revolution', it goes without saying, I was flayed. I'm Chinese. I can't claim to have high political consciousness, but at least I love my country and really want China to become rich and strong. I never dreamed that now that I'm nearing fifty I'd suddenly leave my homeland."

"Do you really have to go?" Lu asked gently.

"Yes. Why? I've debated this with myself many times." Liu shook the half-full cup of red wine he was holding. "I've passed middle age and may not live many years longer. Why should I leave my ashes in a strange land?"

The others listened in silence to this expression of his grief at leaving. Now he suddenly broke off, drained his cup and blurted out, "Go on, curse me! I'm China's unfilial son!"

"Don't say that, Liu. We all know what you've been through." Fu refilled his cup. "Now those dark years are over, the sun is shining again. Everything will change for the better."

"I believe that." Liu nodded. "But when will the sun shine on our family? Shine on our daughter? I can't wait."

"Let's not talk about that." Lu guessed that Liu felt impelled to leave for the sake of his only daughter. Not wanting to go into this, she changed the subject. "I never drink, but today before you and Yafen leave I want to drink to you."

"No, we should drink to *you*." Liu put down his cup. "You're the mainstay of our hospital, one of China's up-and-coming doctors!"

"You're drunk," she laughed.

"I'm not."

Jiang, who had been keeping quiet, now raised her cup and said, "I drink to you from the bottom of my heart! To our twenty-odd years of friendship, and to our future eye-specialist!"

"Goodness! You're talking nonsense! Who am I?" Lu brushed aside this compliment.

"Who are you?" Liu was really half tipsy. "You live in cramped quarters and slave away regardless of criticism, not seeking fame or money. A hard-working doctor like you is an ox serving the children, as Lu Xun said, eating grass and providing milk. Isn't that right, Old Fu?"

Fu drank in silence and nodded.

"There are many people like that, I'm not the only one," Lu demurred with a smile.

"That's why ours is a great nation!" Liu drained another cup.

Jiang glanced at Xiaojia sound asleep on the bed, and said sympathetically, "Yes, you're too busy attending to your patients to nurse your own little girl."

Liu stood up to fill all the cups and declared, "She's sacrificing herself to save mankind."

"What's come over you today, boosting me like this?" Lu wagged a finger at Fu. "You ask him if I'm not selfish, driving my husband into the kitchen and turning my children into ragamuffins. I've messed up the whole family. The fact is, I'm neither a good wife nor mother."

"You're a good doctor!" Liu cried.

Fu took another sip of wine, then put down his cup and commented, "I think your hospital is to blame. Doctors have homes and children like everyone else. And their children may fall ill. Why does no one show any consideration for them?"

"Fu!" Liu cut in loudly. "If I were Director Zhao, I'd first give you a medal, and one each to Yuanyuan and Xiaojia. You're the ones victimized to provide our hospital with such a fine doctor. . . ."

Fu interrupted, "I don't want a medal or a citation. I just wish your hospital understood how hard it is to be a doctor's husband. As soon as the order comes to go out on medical tours or relief work, she's up and off, leaving the family. She comes back so exhausted from the operating theatre, she can't raise a finger to cook a meal. That being the case, if I don't go into the kitchen, who will? I should really be grateful to the 'cultural revolution' for giving me all that time to learn to cook."

"Yafen said long ago that your 'bookworm' label should be torn off." Liu patted his shoulder and laughed. "You can study one of the most advanced branches of science for space travel, and put on a stunning performance in the kitchen — you're becoming one of the new men of the communist era. Who says the achievements of the 'cultural revolution' were not the main aspect of it?"

Fu normally never drank. Today after a few cups his face was red. He caught hold of Liu's sleeve and chuckled, "Right, the 'cultural revolution' was a great revolution to remould us. Didn't those few years change me into a male housewife? If you don't believe it, ask Wenting. Didn't I turn my hand to every chore?"

This embittered joking upset Lu. But she could not stop them. It seemed this was now the only way to lessen their grief at parting. She forced herself to smile back at her husband.

"You learned to do everything except sew cloth shoe-soles. That's why Yuanyuan keeps clamouring for a pair of gym-shoes."

"You expect too much," said Liu with a straight face. "However thoroughly Fu remoulds himself, he can't turn into an old village woman carrying a shoe-sole around everywhere!"

"If the 'gang of four' hadn't been smashed, I might really have carried a shoe-sole to the criticism meetings in my institute," said Fu. "Just think, if things had gone on like that, science, technology and learning would all have been scrapped, leaving nothing but sewing cloth shoe-soles."

But how long could they keep up these wry jokes? They talked of the springtime of science since the overthrow of the gang, of the improved political status of intellectuals although they were underpaid, of the difficulties of middle-aged professionals. The atmosphere became heavy again.

"Old Liu, you have lots of contacts, it's too bad you're leaving." Fu roused himself to slap Liu on the back. "I hear home helps get very well paid. I'd like you to find me a place as a male domestic."

"My leaving doesn't matter," Liu retorted. "Just put an ad in that new paper *The Market*."

"That's a good idea!" Fu adjusted his thick-rimmed glasses. "The advertiser is a university graduate with a mastery of two foreign languages. A good cook, tailor and washerman, able to do both skilled and heavy work. His health is sound, his temper good, he's bold, hard-working and willing to accept criticism. And, last of all, his wages can be settled at the interview." He laughed.

Jiang was sitting quietly, neither eating nor drinking. Watching them laugh, she wanted to join in but could not. She nudged her husband.

"Don't talk like that, what's the point?"

"This is a widespread social phenomenon, that's the point." Liu made a sweeping gesture. "Middle age, middle age. Everyone agrees that middle-aged cadres are the backbone of our country. The operations in a hospital depend on middle-aged surgeons; the most important research projects are thrust on middle-aged scientists and technicians; the hardest jobs in industry are given to middle-aged workers; the chief courses in school are taught by middle-aged teachers. . . ."

"Don't go on and on!" Jiang put in. "Why should a doctor worry about all that?"

Liu screwed up his eyes and continued half tipsy, "Didn't Lu You say, 'Though in a humble position I remain concerned for my country?' I'm a doctor no one has ever heard of, but I keep affairs of state in mind. Everyone acknowledges the key role of the middle-aged, but who knows how hard their life is? At work they shoulder a heavy load, at home they have all the housework. They have to support their parents and bring up their children. They play a key role not just because of their experience and ability, but because they put up with hardships and make great sacrifices — as do their wives and children."

Lu had listened blankly. Now she interposed softly, "It's a pity so few people realize that." Fu, who had been speechless, filled Liu's cup and declared cheerfully, "You should have studied sociology."

Liu laughed sarcastically. "If I had, I'd have been a big Rightist! Sociologists have to study social evils."

"If you uncover them and set them right, society can make progress. That's to the left not the right," said Fu.

"Never mind, I don't want to be either. But I really am interested in social problems. For instance, the problem of the middle-aged." Liu rested his elbows on the table, toying with his empty cup, and began again, "There used to be a saying, 'At middle age a man gives up all activities.' That was true in the old society when people aged prematurely. By forty they felt they were old. But now that saying should be changed to 'At middle age a man is frantically busy!' Right? This reflects the fact that in our new society people are younger, full of vitality. Middle age is a time to give full play to one's abilities."

"Well said!" Fu approved.

"Don't be in such a hurry to express approval. I've another crazy notion." Liu gripped Fu's arm and continued eagerly, "Looking at it that way, you can say our middle-aged generation is lucky to be alive at this time. But in fact we're an unlucky generation."

"You're monopolizing the conversation!" protested Jiang.

But Fu said, "I'd like to hear why we're unlucky."

"Unlucky because the time when we could have done our best work was disrupted by Lin Biao and the 'gang of four'," Liu sighed. "Take your case, you nearly became an unemployed vagrant. Now we middle-aged people are the ones chiefly responsible for modernization, and we don't feel up to it. We haven't the knowledge, energy or strength. We're overburdened — that's our tragedy."

"There's no pleasing you!" laughed Jiang. "When you're not used, you complain that your talents are wasted, you live at the wrong time. When you're fully used, you gripe that you're overworked and underpaid!"

"Don't you ever complain?" her husband retorted.

Jiang hung her head and did not answer.

All Liu had said had given Lu the impression that he felt impelled to leave not entirely for his daughter's sake, but also for his own.

Once more Liu raised his cup and cried, "Come on! Let's drink to middle age!"

10

After their guests had gone and the children were asleep, Lu washed up in the kitchen. In their room, she found her husband, leaning against the bed, deep in thought, his hand on his forehead.

"A penny for them, Jiajie." Lu was surprised he looked so depressed.

Fu asked in reply, "Do you remember Petöfi's poem?"

"Of course!"

"I wish I were a crumbling ruin. . . ." Fu removed

his hand from his forehead. "I'm a ruin now, like an old man. Going bald and grey. I can feel the lines on my forehead. I'm a ruin!"

He did look older than his age. Upset, Lu touched his forehead. "It's my fault! We're such a burden to you!"

Fu took her hand and held it lovingly. "No. You're not to blame."

"I'm a selfish woman, who thinks only about her work." Lu's voice quivered. She couldn't take her eyes away from his forehead. "I have a home but I've paid it little attention. Even when I'm not working, my mind is preoccupied with my patients. I haven't been a good wife or mother."

"Don't be silly! I know more than anyone how much you've sacrificed!" He stopped as tears welled up in his eyes.

Nestling up against him, she said sadly, "You've aged. I don't want you to grow old. . . ."

"Never mind. 'If my love green ivy would be, she'd tenderly entwine around my lonely head.'" Softly he recited their favourite poem.

In the still autumn night, Lu fell asleep against her husband's chest, her lashes moist with tears. Fu put her carefully on the bed. Opening her eyes she asked, "Did I fall asleep?"

"You're very tired."

"No. I'm not."

Fu propped himself up and said to her, "Even metal has fatigue. A microscopic crack is formed first, and it develops until a fracture suddenly occurs."

That was Fu's field of research, and he often mentioned it. But this time, his words carried weight and left a deep impression on Lu.

A dreadful fatigue, a dreadful fracture. In the quiet of the night, Lu seemed to hear the sound of breaking. The props of heavy bridges, sleepers under railways, old bricks and the ivy creeping up ruins . . . all these were breaking.

II

The night deepened.

The pendent lamp in the room having been turned off, the wall lamp shed a dim blue light.

Before her eyes flitted two blue dots of light, like fireflies on a summer night or a will-o'-the-wisp in the wilderness, which turned into Qin's cold stare when she looked carefully.

Qin, however, had been warm and kind when she summoned Lu to Jiao's room the morning he entered the hospital. "Sit down please, Dr Lu. Old Jiao has gone to have his ECG done. He'll be back in a minute."

All smiles, she had risen from an armchair in a room in a quiet building with red-carpeted corridors reserved for high cadres.

Qin had asked her to sit in the other armchair, while she went over to the locker beside the bed and got out a basket of tangerines, which she placed on the side table between the chairs.

"Have a tangerine."

Lu declined. "No, thank you."

"Try one. They were sent to me by a friend in the

south. They're very good." She took one and offered it to her.

Lu took it, but held it in her hand. Qin's new friendliness sent a chill down her spine. She was still conscious of the coldness in Qin's eyes when they had first met.

"What actually is a cataract, Dr Lu? Some doctors told me that an operation is not suitable for all cases." Qin's manner was humble and ingratiating.

"A growth which progressively covers the eyeball, destroying the sight." Looking at the tangerine in her hand, Lu explained, "It can be divided into stages. It's better to have the operation done when the cataract is mature."

"I see. What happens if it isn't done then?"

"The lens shrinks as the cortex is absorbed. The suspensory ligament becomes fragile. The difficulty of the operation increases as the lens is liable to be dislocated."

Qin nodded.

She had not understood nor tried to understand what she had been told. Lu wondered why she had bothered to ask questions. Just passing time? Having started her ward duty only that morning, she had to familiarize herself with the cases of her patients and attend to them. She couldn't sit there, making small talk. She wanted to check Jiao's eyes if he returned soon.

Qin had more questions for her. "I heard there was an artificial lens abroad. The patient needn't wear a convex lens after an operation. Is that right?"

Lu nodded. "We're experimenting on that too."

Qin inquired eagerly, "Can you put one in for my husband?"

Lu smiled. "I said it's still at the experimental stage. I don't think he'd want one now, do you?"

"No." Of course she didn't want him to be a guinea-pig. "What is the procedure for his operation?"

Lu was baffled. "What do you mean?"

"Shouldn't you map out a plan in case something unexpected crops up?" As Lu looked blank, she added, "I've often read about it in the papers. Sometimes surgeons form a team to discuss and work out a plan."

Lu couldn't help laughing. "No need for that! This is a very simple operation."

Disgruntled, Qin looked away. Then she turned back and pressed her point patiently with a smile, "Underestimating the enemy often leads to failure. This has happened in the history of our Party." Then she got Lu to describe certain situations which could cause the operation to fail.

"One has to think twice about patients with heart trouble, hypertension or bronchitis. Coughing can create problems."

"That's just what I feared," Qin cried, striking the arm of her chair. "My husband's heart isn't good and he has high blood pressure."

"We always examine the patient thoroughly before an operation," Lu consoled her.

"He has bronchitis too."

"Has he been coughing lately?"

"No. But what if he does on the operating-table? What shall we do?"

Why was she so anxious, Lu wondered, looking at her watch. The morning was almost gone. Her glance fell on the white lace curtain hanging beside the French windows and tension gripped her when the footsteps approaching the door moved away again. After a long time, Jiao, a blue and white dressing-gown round his shoulders, was helped in by a nurse.

Qin commented, "It's taken you a long time!"

Jiao shook Lu's hand and flopped down exhausted in the armchair. "There were lots of examinations. I had a blood test, an X-ray, and an ECG. The staff were all very kind to me. I didn't have to wait my turn."

He sipped the cup of tea Qin handed him. "I never thought an eye operation involved so many tests."

Lu read the reports. "The X-ray and the ECG are normal. Your blood pressure's a bit high."

Qin piped up. "How high?"

"150 over 100. But that doesn't matter." Then she asked, "Have you been coughing recently, Vice-minister Jiao?"

"No," he answered lightly.

Qin pressed, "Can you guarantee that you won't cough on the operating-table?"

"Well...." Jiao was not so sure.

"That's important, Old Jiao," Qin warned him gravely. "Dr Lu just told me that if you cough, the eyeball can fall out."

Jiao turned to Lu. "How can I be certain I won't cough?"

"It's not that serious. If you are a smoker, don't smoke before the operation."

"OK."

Qin pressed again. "But what if you should cough? What will happen?"

Lu laughed. "Don't worry, Comrade Qin. We can sew up the incision and open it again after he stops coughing."

"That's right," said Jiao. "When I had my right eye operated on, it was sewn up and then opened again. But it wasn't because I coughed!"

Curiosity made Lu ask, "Why then?"

Jiao put down his cup and took out his cigarette case, but put it away again remembering Lu's advice. With a sigh he related, "I'd been labelled as a traitor and was having a difficult time. When the sight went in my right eye I had an operation. Soon after it started, the rebels came and tried to force the surgeon not to treat me. I nearly choked with indignation, but the doctor calmly sewed up the incision, threw the rebels out and then removed the cataract."

"Really?" Stunned, Lu asked, "Which hospital was that?"

"This one."

A coincidence? She looked at Jiao again to see whether she had seen him before, but could not recognize him.

Ten years ago, she had been operating on a so-called traitor when she had been interrupted by some rebels. That patient's name was Jiao. So it was he! Later, the rebels from Jiao's department, collaborating with a rebel in the hospital, put up a slogan claiming that "Lu Wenting betrays the proletariat by operating on the traitor Jiao Chengsi".

No wonder she hadn't recognized him. Ten years ago, Jiao, sallow and depressed, dressed in an old cotton-padded coat, had come to the hospital alone as ordinary patient. Lu suggested an operation and made an appointment, which he kept. When she began operating she heard the nurse saying outside, "No admittance. This is the operating theatre."

Then she heard shouting and noises. "Shit! He's a traitor. We're against treating traitors."

"We won't allow stinking intellectuals to treat traitors."

"Force open the door!"

Jiao, indignant, said on the operating-table, "Let me go blind, doctor. Don't do it."

Lu warned him against moving and quickly sewed up the incision.

Three men charged in, while the more timid ones hesitated at the door. Lu sat there immobile.

Jiao said the doctor had thrown them out. As a matter of fact, Lu had not. She had sat on the stool by the operating-table in her white gown, green plastic slippers, blue cap and mask. All that could be seen of her were her eyes and her bare arms above the rubber gloves. The rebels were awed perhaps by her strange appearance, the solemn atmosphere of the operating theatre and the bloody eye exposed through a hole in the white towel covering the patient. Lu said tersely from behind her mask, "Get out, please!"

The rebels looked at each other and left.

When Lu resumed work, Jiao told her, "Don't do it, doctor, they'll only blind me again even if you cure me. And you may get involved."

"Keep quiet." Lu worked swiftly. When she was bandaging him, all she had said was, "I'm a doctor." That was how it had happened.

The rebels from Jiao's department, coming to the hospital to put up a big-character poster denouncing her for curing a traitor, had created quite a sensation. But what did it matter? She was already being criticized for being a bourgeois specialist. These charges and this operation had not left much impression on her. She had forgotten all about it, until Jiao had brought it up.

"I really respect her, Dr Lu. She was a true doctor," Qin sighed. "Pity the hospital kept no records then. I can't find out who she was. Yesterday I expressed my wish to Director Zhao to have her operate on my husband." Lu's awkward expression made her add, "I'm sorry, Dr Lu. Since Director Zhao has confidence in you, we will too. I hope you won't let him down. Learn from that doctor. Of course, we've a lot to learn from her too, don't you agree?"

Lu had no alternative but to nod.

"You're still young," Qin said encouragingly. "I heard you haven't joined the Party yet. You must strive for it, comrade."

Lu told her frankly, "I don't have a good class background."

"That's not the way to look at things. You can't choose your family but you can choose what you do with your life." Qin was eloquent and enthusiastic. "Our Party does pay attention to class origins, but not exclusively. It's your attitude that counts. When you draw the line between yourself and your family, get close to the Party and make contributions to the people, then the Party will open its doors to you."

Lu crossed the room to draw the curtain and examined Jiao's eye. Then she told Jiao, "If it's all right with you, let's do the operation the day after tomorrow."

Jiao answered briskly, "All right. The earlier the better."

It was already after six when Lu took her leave. Qin hurried out after her. "Are you going home, Dr Lu?"

"Yes."

"Shall I arrange for Jiao's car to take you?"

"No, thank you." Lu declined with a wave of her hand.

12

It was almost midnight, the ward was very quiet. A single wall lamp cast a pale blue light on an intravenous drip, from which the medicine was dropping, as if the only sign of Dr Lu's life.

Fu, sitting at the side of the bed, stared blankly at his wife. It was the first time that he had sat alone with her since her collapse, probably the first time that he had looked at her so intently for the past dozen years.

He remembered that once he had fixed his eyes on her for a long time, and she had asked, her head on one side, "Why do you look at me like that?" Sheepishly he had turned his eyes away. That was when they were courting. But now she could neither move her head nor speak. Vulnerable, she was unable to raise a protest.

Only then did he notice that she looked surprisingly frail and old! Her jet-black hair was streaked with grey; her firm, tender skin, loose and soft; and there were lines on her forehead. The corners of her mouth, once so pretty, were now drooping. Her life, like a dying flame, was petering out fast. He could not believe that his wife, a firm character, had become so feeble overnight!

She was not weak, he knew that well. Slim in build, she was in fact fit and strong. Though her shoulders were slight, she silently endured all hardships and sudden misfortunes. She never complained, feared or became disheartened.

"You're a tough woman," he had often said to her.

"Me? No, I'm timid. Not tough at all." Her answer was always the same.

Only the night before she had fallen ill, she had made, as Fu put it, another "heroic decision" that he should move to his institute.

Xiaojia had quite recovered by then. After Yuanyuan had done his homework, the children went to bed. At last there was peace in the small room.

Autumn had come, the wind was cold. The kindergarten had asked parents for their children's winter clothes. Lu took out the cotton-padded coat Xiaojia had worn the previous year, ripped it apart, made it bigger and sewed on a new pair of cuffs. Then she spread it out on the desk and added a layer of new cotton padding.

Fu took his unfinished article from the bookcase and, hesitating for a brief second beside the desk, sat down on the bed.

"Just a moment," Lu said without turning her head, hurrying, "I'll soon finish."

When she removed the coat from the desk, Fu remarked, "If only we could have another small room. Even six square metres, just big enough for a desk."

Lu listened, lowering her head, busy sewing. After a while, she hastily folded up the unfinished coat and said, "I've got to go to the hospital now. You can have the desk."

"But why? It's late," he queried.

She said, while putting on her jacket, "There will be

two operations tomorrow morning and I want to check how the patients are. I'll go and have a look at them."

She often went to the hospital in the evening in fact. So Fu teased her, saying, "Though you're here at home, your heart's still in the hospital."

"Put on more clothes. It's cold," he urged.

"I won't be long," she said quickly. With an apologetic smile, she continued, "Two funny patients, you know. One's a vice-minister. His wife's been worrying to death about the operation and making an awful fuss. So I must go to see him. The other's a little girl. She told me today that she had a lot of nightmares and slept badly."

"OK, doc!" He smiled. "Get going and come back soon!"

She left. When she returned he was still burning the midnight oil. Not wanting to disturb him, she said after tucking up the children's quilt, "I'm going to bed first."

He looked round, saw she was in bed and again buried himself in his papers and books. But soon he sensed that she had not fallen asleep. Was it perhaps the light? He bent the lamp lower, shielded the light with a newspaper and carried on with his work.

After a while, he heard her soft, even snoring. But he knew that she was faking. Many times, she had tried to pretend she slept well, so he could feel at ease studying late. In fact he had long since seen through her little trick, but had no heart to expose it.

Some time later, he got to his feet, stretched and said, "All right! I'll sleep too."

"Don't worry about me!" Lu said quickly. "I'm already half asleep."

Standing with his hands on the edge of the desk, he

hesitated, looking at his unfinished article. Then he made up his mind and said, closing all the books, "I'll call it a day."

"How about your article? How can you finish it if you don't make full use of your nights?"

"One night can't make up for ten years."

Lu sat up, threw a sweater over her shoulders and said in earnest, her head against the bed board, "Guess what I've been thinking just now?"

"You oughtn't to have thought of anything! Now close *your* eyes. You'll have to cure other people's eyes tomorrow."

"It's no joke. Listen, I think you should move into your institute. Then you'll have more time."

Fu stared at her. Her face was glowing, her eyes dancing. Obviously she was very pleased with the idea.

She went on, "I'm serious. You've things to do. I know, the children and I have been hampering you."

"Come off it! It's not you. . . ."

Lu broke in, "Of course it is! We can't divorce. The children need their father, and a scientist needs his family. However, we must think of some way to turn your eight working hours into sixteen."

"But the children and the housework will all fall on you. That won't do!"

"Why not? Even without you, we can manage."

He listed all the problems, to which she answered one by one. Finally she said, "Haven't you often remarked that I'm a tough woman? I can cope. Your son won't go hungry, your daughter won't be ill-treated."

He was convinced. So they decided to have a try the next day.

"It's so very difficult to do something in China!" Fu

said undressing. "During the war, many old revolution-
aries died for a new China. Now to modernize our
country, again our generation has to make sacrifices
though hardly anyone notices it."

He kept talking to himself like this. When he put
his clothes on the back of a chair and turned to get
into bed, he saw that Lu had fallen asleep. With a faint
smile on her face, she looked pleased with her proposal,
even in her dreams.

But who would imagine their trial would fail on the
very first day?

13

The operations were successful, though Lu's private plan
failed.

That morning when she had entered the ward ten
minutes early as usual, Dr Sun was already there waiting
for her.

"Good morning, Dr Lu," he greeted her, "we've got
a donor's eye today. Can we fit in the corneal transplant?"

"Excellent! We've got a patient who's anxious to have
the operation done as soon as possible," Lu exclaimed
in delight.

"But you already have two operations scheduled for
this morning. Do you think you can manage a third?"

"Sure," she replied, straightening up as if showing
him that she was perfectly capable.

"OK, it's settled then." He had made up his mind.

Holding the arm of Jiang, who had just arrived, Lu
headed for the operating theatre. She was in high

spirits, walking with a spring in her step, as though on an outing.

The operating theatres of this hospital, occupying a whole floor, were large and impressive. The big characters "Operating Theatre" in red paint on the beige glass door were striking. When a wheeled stretcher bearing a patient was pushed through this door, his relatives remained outside, anxiously looking at the mysterious, perhaps even frightening place, as if Death were lurking about inside.

But in fact, the operating theatre was a place of hope. Inside, the walls along the wide corridor were painted a light, agreeable green. Here there were the operating theatres for the various departments. The surgeons, their assistants, anaesthetists and theatre nurses scurried to and fro lightly. No laughter, no chatter. This was the most quiet, most orderly area of the large hospital, into which more than a thousand patients poured every day.

Vice-minister Jiao was brought into one of these theatres, and then put on a high cream-coloured operating-table. His head was covered by a sterilized white towel. There was an olive-shaped hole in it revealing one of his eyes.

Lu already in her overall sat on a stool near the operating-table, her gloved hands raised. The height of the stool was adjustable. Lu, being small, had to raise it whenever she operated. But today, it had already been adjusted. She turned and glanced at Jiang gratefully, realizing she had done it.

A nurse pushed the surgical instrument table nearer to Lu. The adjustable plate was now placed above the patient's chest, within the surgeon's reach.

"Shall we start now?" Lu asked watching Jiao's eye. "Try to relax. We'll first inject a local anaesthetic. Then your eye will feel numb. The operation won't take long."

At this, Jiao suddenly cried out, "Steady on!"

What was wrong? Both Lu and Jiang were taken aback. Jiao pulled away the towel from his face, striving to raise his head. He inquired, pointing at Lu, "It was you, Dr Lu, who operated before on my eye?"

Lu quickly raised her gloved hands lest he touch them. Before she could speak, he went on emotionally, "Yes, it was you. It must have been you! You said the same words. Even your tone and intonation are the same!"

"Yes, it was me," Lu had to admit.

"Why didn't you tell me before? I'm so grateful to you."

"Never mind...." Lu could not find anything else to say. She cast a glance at the towel, beckoned the nurse to change it. Then she said again, "Shall we start, Vice-minister Jiao?"

Jiao sighed. It was hard for him to calm down. Lu had to say in a commanding tone, "Don't move. Don't speak. We'll start now."

She skilfully injected some novocaine into his lower eyelid and began the operation. She had performed such operations umpteen times, but every time she picked up her instruments, she felt like a raw recruit on the battlefield. Lu held out two tapering fingers to pick up a needle-holder which looked like a small pair of scissors. She fixed the needle to the instrument.

"What's the matter?" Jiang asked softly.

Instead of answering, Lu held the hook-shaped needle up to the light to examine it.

"Is this a new one?"

Jiang had no idea, so they both turned to the nurse. "A new needle?"

The nurse stepped forward and said in a low voice, "Yes, a new one."

Lu had another look at the needle pin and grumbled, "How can we use such a needle?"

Lu and some other doctors had complained many times about the poor quality of their surgical instruments. However, faulty ones appeared from time to time. Lu could do nothing about it. When she found good scalpels, scissors and needles, she would ask the nurse to keep them for her for later use.

She had no idea that all the surgical instruments had been replaced by new ones that day, but unfortunately there was a bad needle among them. Whenever such things occurred, Lu's good-natured face would change, and she would reprimand the nurse. The young nurse, though innocent perhaps, could not defend herself. There was nothing to say in the circumstances. A blunt needle not only prolonged the operation, but also increased the patient's suffering.

Frowning, Lu said quietly, so that Jiao could not overhear, "Bring me another!"

It was an order, and the nurse picked out an old needle from a sterilizer.

The theatre nurses respected Lu, while at the same time being afraid of her. They admired her skill and feared her strictness. A doctor's authority was established through his scalpel. A good oculist could give a blind man back his sight, while a bad one might blind him permanently. Lu had no position, no power, but through her scalpel she wielded authority.

The operation was almost complete, when Jiao's body jerked suddenly.

"Don't move!" Lu warned him.

"Don't move!" Jiang repeated quickly. "What's the matter?"

"I . . . want to . . . cough!" a strangled voice sounded from under the towel.

This was just what his wife had feared would happen. Why choose this moment to cough? Was it psychological? A conditioned reflex?

"Can you control it for a minute?"

"No, I . . . I can't." His chest was heaving.

There was no time to lose! Lu hurriedly took emergency measures, while calming him down, "Just a second! Breathe out and hold your cough!"

She was quickly tying up the suture while he exhaled, his chest moving vigorously as if he would die of suffocation at any moment. When the last knot was done, Lu sighed with relief and said, "You can cough now, but not too loudly."

But he did not. On the contrary, his breath gradually grew even and normal.

"Go ahead and cough. It won't matter," Jiang urged again.

"I'm awfully sorry," Jiao apologized. "I'm all right now. Carry on with the operation please."

Jiang rolled her eyes, wanting to give him a piece of her mind. A man of his age should know better. Lu threw her a glance, and Jiang bit back her resentment. They smiled knowingly at each other. It was all in the day's work!

Lu snipped off the knots and started the operation again. It continued without a hitch. Afterwards Lu got off the stool and sat at a small table to write out a prescription, while Jiao was moved back on to the wheeled stretcher. As it was being pushed out, Jiao suddenly called to Lu, like a kid who has misbehaved, his voice trembling slightly.

Lu stepped over to him. His eyes had been bandaged. "Anything I can do?" she stooped to ask.

He reached out, groping. When he caught hold of her hands, still in their gloves, he shook them vigorously. "I've given you much trouble on both occasions. I'm so sorry. . . ."

Lu was stunned for a brief moment. Then she consoled him, looking at his bandaged face, "Never mind. Have a good rest. We'll take off the bandage in a few days."

After he was wheeled out, Lu glanced at the clock. A forty-minute operation had lasted an hour. She took off her white gown and rubber gloves and immediately donned another. As Lu turned to let the nurse tie the gown at the back, Jiang asked, "Shall we continue?"

"Yes."

14

"Let me do the next operation," Jiang begged. "You take a short rest, then do the third."

Lu shook her head and said smilingly, "I'll do it. You're not familiar with Wang Xiaoman. The child's scared stiff. We became friends during the last few days. Better leave her to me."

The girl did not come into the operating theatre on a wheeled stretcher, but was almost dragged in. In a white gown, which was a bit too large for her, she was reluctant to go anywhere near the operating-table.

"Aunt Lu, I'm scared. I don't want the operation. Please go and explain to my mother."

The sight of the doctors and nurses in such strange clothes terrified her. Her heart was pounding, as she tried to wrench away from the nurses, pleading with Lu for help.

Lu walked towards the table and coaxed her with a grin, "Come on, little girl. Didn't you promise to have this operation? Be brave! There's nothing to fear. You won't feel any pain once you've been given some anaesthetic."

Xiaoman sized up Lu in her funny clothes and gazed at her kind, smiling, encouraging eyes. Then she climbed up on to the operating-table. A nurse spread a towel over her face. Lu motioned the nurse to tie up her hands. As the little patient was about to protest, Lu said, perching on the table, "Xiaoman, be a good girl! It's the same for all patients. Really, it won't take long." She gave her an injection of the anaesthetic while telling her, "I'm giving you an injection and soon your eye will feel nothing at all."

Lu was both doctor, devoted mother and kindergarten nurse. She took the scissors, forceps and other instruments which Jiang handed to her while keeping up a running commentary for the benefit of the girl. When she severed the straight muscle which caused the squint, Xiaoman's nerve was affected and she became nauseous.

"You feel a little sick?" Lu asked. "Take a deep breath. Just hold on for a minute. That's better. Still sick? Feeling any better? We'll finish the operation very soon. There's a good girl!"

Lu's words lulled Xiaoman into a trance while the operation continued. When she had been bandaged and wheeled out of the room, she remembered what her mother had told her to say, so she called out sweetly, "Thank you very much, aunty."

Everyone burst out laughing. The minute hand of the clock on the wall had just moved half an hour.

Lu was wet with sweat, the perspiration beading on her forehead, her underwear soaking. Wet patches showed under her armpits. She was surprised at this because it was not hot. Why had she perspired so profusely? She slightly moved her numb arms, which had ached from being raised for the duration of the operation.

When she removed the operating gown again and reached out for another, she suddenly felt dizzy. She closed her eyes for a minute, shook her head several times and then slowly eased one of her arms into a sleeve. A nurse came to help her tie the gown.

"Dr Lu!" the nurse exclaimed suddenly. "Your lips are so pale!"

Jiang, who was also changing, turned to look at Lu. "Goodness!" she said in astonishment. "You do look very pale!"

It was true. There were black rings under her eyes, even her lids were puffy. She looked a patient herself!

Seeing that Jiang's startled eyes remained fixed on her, Lu grinned and said, "Stop fussing! It'll soon be over."

She had no doubt that she could carry on with the next operation. Had she not worked like this for years?

"Shall we continue?" the nurse queried.

"Yes, of course."

How could they afford to stop? The donor's eye could not be stored too long, nor the operation be delayed. They had to go on working.

"Wenting," Jiang stepped over to Lu and suggested, "Let's have a break for half an hour."

Lu looked at the clock. It was just after ten. If they postponed it for half an hour, some colleagues would be late for lunch, while others had to rush home to prepare a meal for their children.

"Continue?" the nurse asked again.

"Yes."

15

Doctors of this and other hospitals who were undergoing further training thronged the door talking to Lu. They had got special permission to see her operate.

Uncle Zhang, helped by a nurse, clambered on to the operating-table, still talking and laughing.

The table was a bit too small for him and his feet and hands dangled over the sides. He had a loud voice and talked incessantly, joking with a nurse, "Don't laugh at me, girl. If the medical team hadn't come to our village and persuaded me to have this operation, I'd rather die than let you cut my eye with a knife. Just imagine! A steel knife cutting into my flesh, ugh! Who knows if it will do me some good or not? Ha! Ha! . . ."

The young nurse tittered and said softly, "Uncle, lower your voice please."

"I know, young lady. We must keep quiet in a hospital, mustn't we?" he still boomed. Gesticulating busily with one hand, he went on, "You can't imagine how

I felt when I heard that my eye could be cured. I wanted to laugh and, at the same time, to cry. My father went blind in his old age and died a blind man. I never dreamed that a blind man like me could see the sun again. Times have really changed, haven't they?"

The nurse giggled while covering him with a towel. "Don't move again, uncle!" she said. "This towel's been sterilized, don't touch it."

"All right," he answered gravely. "Since I'm in hospital, I should obey the rules." But he was trying to raise his strong arms again.

Worrying about his restlessness, the nurse said, holding a strap, "I'll have to tie your arms to the table, uncle. That's the rule here."

Zhang was puzzled, but soon chortled. "Truss me up, eh?" he joked. "OK, go ahead! To be frank, lass, if it were not for my eyes, I wouldn't be so obedient. Though blind, I go to the fields twice a day. I was born a lively character. I like to be on the go. I just can't sit still."

This made the nurse laugh, and he himself chuckled too. But he stopped immediately when Lu entered. He asked, cocking up his ears, "Is that you, Dr Lu? I can recognize your steps. It's funny, since I lost my sight, my ears have grown sharp."

Seeing him full of beans, Lu could not help laughing. She took her seat, preparing for the operation. When she picked up the precious donor's cornea from a phial and sewed it on to a piece of gauze, he piped up again, "So an eye can be replaced? I never knew that!"

"It's not replacing the whole eye, just a filmy membrane," Jiang corrected him.

"Can't see the difference." He wasn't interested in

details. With a sigh, he continued, "It needs much skill, doesn't it? When I return to my village with a pair of good eyes, the villagers'll say I must have met some kind fairy. Ha! Ha! I'll tell them I met Dr Lu!"

Jiang tittered, winking at Lu, who felt a little embarrassed. Still sewing, she explained, "Other doctors can do the same."

"That's quite true," he agreed. "You only find good doctors in this big hospital. No kidding!"

Her preparations over, Lu parted his eyelids with a speculum and said, "We'll start now. Just relax."

Zhang was not like other patients, who only listened to whatever the doctors said. He thought it impolite not to answer. So he said understandingly, "I'm perfectly all right. Go ahead. I don't mind if it's painful. Of course, it hurts to cut with a scalpel or a pair of scissors. But don't worry about me. I trust you. Besides...."

Jiang had to stop him, still smiling. "Uncle, don't talk any more."

Finally he complied.

Lu picked up a trephine, small as a pen cap, and lightly cut out the opaque cornea. Cutting a similar disc of clear cornea from the donor's eye, she transferred it to Zhang's eye. Then she began the delicate task of stitching it with the needle-holder. The suture was finer than a hair.

The operation went smoothly. When she had finished, the transplanted cornea was perfectly fixed on the surface of the eye. But for some little black knots, one could never tell it was a new cornea.

"Well done!" the doctors around the operating-table quietly exclaimed in admiration.

Lu sighed with relief. Deeply touched, Jiang looked up at her friend with feeling. Silently, she put layers of gauze over Zhang's eye. . . .

As he was wheeled out, Zhang seemed to awaken from a dream. He became animated again. When the wheeled stretcher was already out of the door, he cried out, "Thanks a lot, Dr Lu!"

The operations had ended. As Lu was pulling herself to her feet, she found her legs had gone to sleep. She simply could not stand up. After a little rest, she tried again and again, till she finally made it. There was a sudden pain in her side. She pressed it with her hand, not taking it seriously for it had occurred before. Engrossed in an operation, sitting on the little stool, for hours at a time, she was aware of nothing else. But as soon as this operation had ended, she felt utterly exhausted, even too tired to move.

16

At that moment, Fu was cycling home in haste. He had not intended to return that day. Early that morning, Fu, at his wife's suggestion, had rolled up his bedding, put it on his bicycle carrier and taken it to his office to begin his new life.

By noon, however, he was wavering. Would Lu finish her operations in time? Imagining her dragging herself home to prepare lunch for the children, he suddenly felt a pang of guilt. So he jumped on his bicycle and pedalled home.

Just as he turned into their lane, he caught sight of his wife leaning against a wall, unable to move.

"Wenting! What's wrong?" he cried out, leaping off to help.

"Nothing. I'm just a bit tired." She put an arm round his shoulder and moved slowly towards home.

Fu noticed that she was very pale and that beads of cold sweat had broken out on her forehead.

He asked uneasily, "Shall I take you to hospital?"

She sat down on the edge of the bed, her eyes closed, and answered, "Don't worry. I'll be all right after a short rest."

She pointed to the bed, too weak to say anything. Fu took off her shoes and coat.

"Lie down and get some sleep. I'll wake you later."

He went to boil some water in a saucepan. When he came back to fetch noodles, he heard her say, "We ought to have a rest. Shall we take the children to Beihai Park next Sunday? We haven't been there for more than ten years."

"Fine. I'm all for it!" Fu agreed, wondering why she should suddenly want to go there.

He gave her an anxious glance and went to cook the noodles. When he returned, food in hand, she had already fallen asleep. He did not disturb her. When Yuanyuan came home, the two of them sat down to eat.

Just then, Lu began groaning. Fu put down his bowl and rushed to the bed. Lu was deathly white, her face covered in sweat.

"I can't fight it," she said in a feeble voice, gasping for breath.

Frightened, Fu took her hand asking, "What's wrong? Have you any pain?"

With a great effort, Lu pointed to her heart.

Panicking, Fu pulled open a drawer rummaging for

a pain-killer. On second thoughts, he wondered if she needed a tranquillizer.

Though in great pain, she was clear-headed. She signed to him to calm down and said with all her remaining strength, "I must go to hospital!"

Only then did Fu realize the seriousness of her illness. For more than ten years she had never seen a doctor, though she went to the hospital every day. Now she was obviously critically ill. As he hurried out, he stopped at the door and turned to say, "I'll go and get a taxi."

He rushed to the public telephone on the corner. He dialled quickly and waited. When someone answered, he heard a cold voice saying, "No taxis at the moment."

"Look, I've got a very sick person here!"

"Still, you'll have to wait half an hour."

Fu began to plead, when the man rang off.

He tried to call Lu's hospital, but no one seemed to be in the office of the Ophthalmic Department. He asked the operator to put him through to the vehicle dispatch office.

"We can't send you a car without an official approval slip," was the answer.

Where on earth could he track down the hospital leaders to get an approval slip?

"But this is urgent! Hello!" he shouted into the receiver. But the line had already gone dead.

He phoned the political department which, he thought, ought to help him out. After a long time, a woman picked up the receiver. She listened patiently and said politely, "Would you please contact the administration department?"

He had to ask the operator to put him through to the administration department. Recognizing his voice, the operator demanded impatiently, "Where exactly do you want?"

Where? He was not sure himself. In a begging voice, he said he wanted to speak to anyone in the administration department. The telephone rang and rang. Nobody answered.

Disappointed, Fu abandoned the idea of finding a car. He headed for a small workshop in the lane making cardboard boxes, hoping to borrow a tricycle and trailer. The old lady in charge, hearing of his predicament, sympathized with him, but unfortunately could do nothing, for both her tricycles were out.

What was to be done? Standing in the alley, Fu was desperate. Sit Lu on the bicycle carrier? That was impossible.

Just then, Fu saw a van coming. Without much thought, he raised his hand to stop it.

The van came to a halt, and the driver poked his head out, staring in surprise. But when he heard what was happening, he beckoned Fu to get into the van.

They went straight to Fu's home. When the driver saw Lu being dragged towards the van supported by her husband, he hurried to help her get into the cabin. Then slowly he drove her to the casualty department of the hospital.

17

She had never slept so long, never felt so tired. She felt pain all over her body as if she had just fallen from a cloud. She had not the slightest bit of strength left. After a peaceful sleep, her limbs were more relaxed, her heart calmer. But she felt her mind go blank.

For years, she had simply had no time to pause, to reflect on the hardships she had experienced or the difficulties lying ahead. Now all physical and mental burdens had been lifted. She seemed to have plenty of time to examine her past and to explore the future. But her mind had switched off; no reminiscences, no hopes. Nothing.

Perhaps it was only a dream. She had had such dreams before. . . .

One evening when she was only five, a north wind had been howling. Her mother had gone out, leaving her alone at home. Soon it was very dark and her mother had not returned. For the first time, Lu felt lonely, terrified. She cried and shouted, "Mama . . . mama. . . ." This scene often appeared later in her dreams. The howling wind, the door blown open by a sudden gust and the pale kerosene lamp remained vividly in her mind. For a long time, she could not tell whether it had been true or a dream.

This time, it was not a dream but reality.

She was in bed, ill, and Jiajie was attending her. He looked flaked out too. He was dozing, half lying on the bed. He would catch cold if not awakened. She tried to call him, but no sound came out of her mouth. There was a lump in her throat choking her. She wanted to pull a coat over him, but her arms did not seem to belong to her.

She glanced round and saw she was in a single room. Only serious cases were given such special treatment. She was suddenly seized by fear. "Am I. . . ?"

The autumn wind rattled the door and windows. Darkness gathered, swallowing up the room. Lu felt clearer after a cold sweat. It was real, she knew, not a dream. This was the end of life, the beginning of death!

So this was dying, no fear, no pain, just life withering away, the senses blurring, slowly sinking, like a leaf drifting on a river.

All came to an end, inevitably. Rolling waves swept over her chest. Lu felt she was floating in the water. . . .

"Mama . . . mama. . . ."

She heard Xiaojia's call and saw her running along the bank. She turned back, reaching out her arms.

"Xiaojia . . . my darling daughter. . . ."

But waves swept her away, and Xiaojia's face grew vague, her hoarse voice turned into sobbing.

"Mama . . . plait my hair. . . ."

Why not plait her hair? The child had been in this world for six years, and her one desire was to have pigtails. Whenever she saw other girls with pigtails adorned with silk ribbons, admiration overwhelmed her little heart. But such requests were ignored. Mother had no time for that. On Monday morning, the hospital was crowded with patients and, for Lu, every minute counted.

"Mama . . . mama. . . ."

She heard Yuanyuan's calling and saw the boy running after her along the bank. She turned back, stretching out her arms.

"Yuanyuan . . . Yuanyuan. . . ."

A wave swept over her. When she struggled to the surface, there was no sign of her son, only his voice in the distance.

"Mama . . . don't forget . . . my white gym shoes. . . ."

A kaleidoscope of sports shoes whirled around. White

and blue sneakers, sports boots, gym shoes, white shoes with red or blue bands. Buy a pair for Yuanyuan, whose shoes were already worn out. Buy a pair of white gym shoes and he would be in raptures for a month. But then the shoes disappeared and raining down were price tags: 3.1 yuan, 4.5 yuan, 6.3 yuan. . . .

Now she saw Jiajie chasing after her, his running figure mirrored in the water. He was in a great hurry, his voice trembling as he called, "Wenting, you can't leave us like this!"

How she wished that she could wait for him! He held out his hand to her, but the ruthless current raced forward and she drifted away helplessly.

"Dr Lu . . . Dr Lu . . . ."

So many people were calling her, lining the banks. Yafen, Old Liu, Director Zhao, Dr Sun, all in white coats; Jiao Chengsi, Uncle Zhang and Wang Xiaoman in pyjamas. Among the other patients, she only recognized a few. They were all calling her.

I oughtn't to leave. No! There are so many things I still have to do. Xiaojia and Yuanyuan shouldn't be motherless. I mustn't bring Jiajie more sorrow. He can't afford to lose his wife so young. I can't tear myself away from the hospital, the patients. Oh no! I can't give up this miserable, yet dear life!

I won't drown! I must fight! I must remain in the world. But why am I so tired? I've no strength to resist, to struggle. I'm sinking, sinking. . . .

Ah! Goodbye, Yuanyuan! Goodbye, Xiaojia! Will you miss your mother? In this last moment of my life, I love you more than ever. Oh, how I love you! Let me embrace you. Listen, my darlings, forgive your mummy who did not give you the love you deserved. Forgive your mummy who, time and again, refrained from hugging you, pushing away your smiling faces. Forgive your mummy for leaving you while you're still so small.

Goodbye, Jiajie! You gave up everything for me! Without you, I couldn't have achieved anything. Without you, life had no meaning. Ah, you sacrificed so much for me! If I could, I would kneel down before you begging your pardon since I can never repay all your kindness and concern. Forgive me for neglecting you. I often thought I should do something more for you. I wanted to end my work regularly and prepare supper for you. I wanted to let you have the desk, hoping you would finish your article. But it's too late! How sad! I've no time now.

Goodbye, my patients! For the past eighteen years, my life was devoted to you. Whether I walked, sat or lay down, I thought only of you and your eyes! You don't know the joy I felt after curing an eye. What a pity I shall no longer feel that. . . .

18

"Arrhythmia!" the doctor monitoring the screen exclaimed.

"Wenting! Wenting!" Fu cried out, fixing his eyes on his wife, who was struggling for breath.

The doctors and nurses on duty rushed into the room.

"Intravenous injection of lidocaine!" the doctor snapped an order.

A nurse quickly injected it, but before it was finished, Lu's lips went blue, her hands clenched, her eyes rolled upwards.

Her heart stopped beating.

The doctors began massage resuscitation. A respirator was applied to her head, which made a rhythmic sound. Then a defibrillator went into operation. When her chest was struck by this, her heart began to beat again.

"Get the ice cap ready!" the doctor in charge ordered, the sweat on his forehead.

An ice cap was put on Lu's head.

19

The pale dawn could be seen outside the window. Day had broken at last. Lu had lived through a crucial night. She now entered a new day.

A day nurse came into the room and opened the windows, letting in fresh air and the birds' merry singing. At once the pungent smell of medicine and death were dispelled. Dawn brought new hope to a frail life.

Another nurse came to take Lu's temperature, while a medical orderly brought in breakfast. Then the doctor on duty dropped in on his ward round.

Wang Xiaoman, still bandaged, pleaded with a nurse, "Let me have a look at Dr Lu! Just one peep."

"No. She nearly died last night. No one's allowed to see her for the time being."

"Aunt, perhaps you don't know, but she fell ill because she operated on me. Please let me go and see her. I promise not to say a word to her."

"No, no, no!" The nurse scowled.

"Oh please! Just one glance." Xiaoman was close to tears. Hearing footsteps behind her, she turned and saw Old Zhang coming, led by his grandson.

"Grandpa," she rushed to him, "will you have a word with this aunt? She won't let me...."

Zhang, with his eyes bandaged, was dragged over by the little girl to the nurse.

"Sister, do let us have a look at her."

Now with this old man pestering her too, the nurse flared up, "What's the matter with you people, fooling about in the wards?"

"Come off it! Don't you understand?" Zhang's voice was not so loud today. He went on humbly, "We've a good reason, you know. Why is Dr Lu ill? Because she operated on us. To be frank, I can't really see her, but to stand beside her bed for a while will calm my nerves."

He was so sincere that the nurse softened and explained patiently, "It's not that I'm being mean. Dr Lu's seriously ill with heart trouble. She mustn't be excited. You want her to recover very soon, don't you? Better not disturb her at the moment."

"Yes, you're quite right." Zhang sighed and sat down on a bench. Slapping his thigh, he said regretfully, "It's all my fault. I urged her to do the operation as quickly as possible. But who would've thought. . .? What shall I do if anything happens to her?" He lowered his head in remorse.

Dr Sun hurried to see Lu too before starting his work, but was stopped by Xiaoman.

"Dr Sun, are you going to see Dr Lu?" she asked.

He nodded.

"Will you take me along? Please."

"Not now. Some time later. OK?"

Hearing Sun's voice, Zhang stood up and reached out for him. Tugging Sun's sleeve, he said, "Dr Sun. We'll do as you say. But can I have a word with you? I know you're extremely busy. But I still want you to listen to what's been bothering me."

Sun patted Zhang on the shoulder and said, "Go ahead."

"Dr Lu's a very good doctor. You leaders ought to do your best to cure her. If you save her, she can save many others. There are good medicines, aren't there? Give her them. Don't hesitate. I hear you have to pay for certain precious medicines. Lu's got two children. She's not well off. Now she's ill. I don't expect she can afford them. Can't this big hospital subsidize her?"

He stopped, holding Sun's hands, slightly cocking his ear towards him, waiting for his answer.

Sun had a one-track mind. He never showed his feelings. But today he was moved. Shaking Zhang's hands, he said emotionally, "We'll do everything possible to save her!"

Zhang seemed satisfied. He called his grandson to come nearer, and groped for a satchel which was slung across the boy's shoulder.

"Here are some eggs. Please take them to her when you go in."

"It's not necessary," Sun replied quickly.

This put Zhang's back up instantly. Gripping Sun's hands, he raised his voice, "If you don't take them to her, I won't let you go!"

Sun had to accept the satchel of eggs. He decided to ask a nurse to return it and explain later. As though guessing what was in Sun's mind, Zhang continued, "And don't ask someone to bring them back."

Forced to acquiesce, Sun helped Zhang and Xiaoman down the stairs.

Qin, accompanied by Director Zhao, approached Lu's room. "Zhao," the woman talked while walking, rather excitedly, "I was like a bureaucrat. I didn't know it was Dr Lu who had operated on Old Jiao. But you should have known, shouldn't you? Luckily Jiao recognized Lu. Otherwise we'd still be in the dark."

"I was sent to work in the countryside at that time," Zhao replied helplessly.

Shortly after they had entered the room, Sun arrived. The doctor on duty gave a brief report of the emergency measures taken to save Lu the previous night. Zhao looked over the case-history, nodding. Then he said, "We must watch her carefully."

Fu, seeing so many people entering, had stood up. But Qin, unaware of his presence, quickly sat down on the vacant stool.

"Feeling better, Dr Lu?" she asked.

Lu's eyes opened slightly but she said nothing.

"Vice-minister Jiao has told me all about you," Qin said warmly. "He's very grateful to you. He would have come himself if I hadn't stopped him. I'm here to thank you on his behalf. Anything you fancy eating, anything you want, let me know. I can help you. Don't stand on ceremony. We're all revolutionary comrades."

Lu closed her eyes.

"You're still young. Be optimistic. Since you're sick, it's better to accept it. This. . . ."

Zhao stopped her by saying, "Comrade Qin Bo, let her have some rest. She's only just regained consciousness."

"Fine, fine. Have a good rest," Qin said rising to her feet. "I'll come again in a couple of days."

Out of the ward, Qin complained frowning, "Director Zhao, I must give you a piece of my mind. Dr Lu's a real treasure. If you had been more concerned about her, she wouldn't have become so ill. The middle-aged comrades are the backbone of our country. It's imperative to value talented people."

"Right," was Zhao's reply.

Gazing after her receding figure, Fu asked Sun in a small voice, "Who's she?"

Sun looked over the frame of his spectacles at the doorway and answered frowning, "An old lady spouting revolutionary phrases!"

20

That day, Lu was slightly better and could open her eyes easily. She drank two spoonfuls of milk and a sip of orange juice. But she lay with her eyes blank, staring at the ceiling. She wore a vacant expression, as if indifferent to everything, including her own critical condition and the unhappiness of her family. She seemed weary of life.

Fu stared at her in mute horror for he had never seen her like this before. He called her again and again, but she only responded with a slight wave of her hand, as though not wishing to be disturbed. Probably she felt comfortable letting her mind remain suspended.

Time passed unheeded. Fu, sitting at her bedside, had not slept for two nights. He felt exhausted. Dozing, he was suddenly awoken by a heart-rending scream, which shook the whole ward. He heard a girl wailing next door, "Mama! Mama!" and a man's sobbing. Then there came the sound of footsteps as many people rushed to the room. Fu hurried out too. He saw a wheeled stretcher being pushed out of the room, on which lay a corpse covered with a sheet. Then the nurse in white pushing the stretcher appeared. A girl of sixteen with dishevelled hair stumbled out, shaking, and threw herself at the stretcher. Clutching at it with trembling hands, she pleaded, tears streaming down her cheeks, "Don't take it away! Please! My mother's asleep. She'll soon wake up! I know she will!"

Visitors made way for the wheeled stretcher. In silence, they paid their respects to the deceased.

Fu stood rooted amid the crowd. His cheekbones stuck out prominently in his haggard face. His bloodshot eyes began to fill with tears. Clenching his fists, he tried to pull himself together, but shook all over. Unnerved by the girl's shrill cries, he wanted to cover his ears.

"Mama, wake up! Wake up! They're taking you away!" the girl screamed madly. Had she not been held back by others, she would have pulled off the sheet. The middle-aged man following the stretcher repeated, sobbing, "I've let you down! I've let you down!"

His desperate cries were like a knife piercing Fu's heart, as he stared at the stretcher. All of a sudden, as if electrified, he dashed towards his wife's room. He went straight to her, threw himself on the bed. He murmured with closed eyes, "You're alive!"

Lu stirred awakened by his heavy breathing. She opened her eyes and looked at him, but her eyes didn't seem to focus.

He felt a shiver of fear and cried out, "Wenting!" Her eyes lingered on his face coldly, and this made his heart bleed. Fu did not know what to say or do to encourage her to hold on to life. This was his wife, the dearest person in the world. How long ago was it since he had read poems to her in Beihai Park that winter? During all these years, she had always been his beloved. Life would be unthinkable without her! He must keep her with him!

Poetry! Read a poem to her as he had done then! It was poetry which had helped him to win her before! Today, he would recite the same poem to remind her of sweet memories, to give her the courage to live on.

Half-kneeling beside her bed, he began to recite with tears in his eyes:

> "I wish I were a rapid stream,
> . . . . . .
> If my love
> A tiny fish would be,
> She'd frolic
> In my foaming waves."

The verses seemed to have touched her. She turned her head towards him, her lips moving slightly. Fu leaned over and listened to her indistinct words: "I can no longer . . . swim. . . ."

Choking back his tears, he continued:

> "I wish I were a deserted forest,
> . . . . . .
> If my love
> A little bird would be,
> She'd nest and twitter
> In my dense trees."

She murmured softly, "I can no longer . . . fly. . . ."

His heart ached. Steeling himself, he went on, in tears:

> "I wish I were a crumbling ruin,
> . . . . . .
> If my love
> Green ivy would be,
> She'd tenderly entwine
> Around my lonely head."

Tears, blind tears silently poured down her cheeks and fell on the white pillow. With an effort, she said, "I can't . . . climb up!"

Fu threw himself on to her, weeping bitterly. "I've failed you as a husband. . . ."

When he opened his tearful eyes, he was astonished. Again she remained with her eyes fixed on the ceiling. She seemed unaware of his weeping, his appeals, unaware of everything around her.

On hearing Fu's sobbing, a doctor hurried in and said to him, "Dr Lu's very weak. Please don't excite her."

Fu said nothing more the whole afternoon. At dusk, Lu seemed a little better. She turned her head to Fu and her lips moved as if wanting to speak.

"Wenting, what do you want to say? Tell me," Fu asked, holding her hands.

She spoke at last, "Buy Yuanyuan . . . a pair of white gym shoes. . . ."

"I'll do it tomorrow," he replied, unable to check his tears. But he quickly wiped them away with the back of his hand.

Lu, still watching him, seemed to have more to say.

But she only uttered a few words after a long time, "Plait . . . Xiaojia's hair. . . ."

"Yes, I will!" Fu promised, still sobbing. He looked at his wife, his vision blurred, hoping she would be able to tell him all that was worrying her. But she closed her lips, as if she had used up her energy.

21

Two days later, a letter came for Lu, posted at Beijing International Airport. Fu opened it and read:

Dear Wenting,

I wonder if you will ever receive this letter. It's not impossible that this won't reach you. But I hope not! I don't believe it will happen. Though you're very ill, I believe you'll recover. You can still do a lot. You're too young to leave us!

When my husband and I came to say goodbye to you last night, you were still unconscious. We'd wanted to see you this morning, but there were too many things to do. Yesterday evening may be the last time we will meet. Thinking of this, my heart breaks. We've been studying and working together for more than twenty years. No one understands us as well as we do each other. Who would imagine we would part like this?

I'm now writing this letter in the airport. Can you guess where I'm standing at this moment? At the arts and crafts counter on the second floor. There's no one about, only the shining glass counter in front of me. Remember the first time we travelled by air, we came here too? There was a pot of artificial narcissuses with dew on their petals, so lifelike, so exquisite! You told me that you liked it best. But when we looked at the price, we were scared off. Now, I'm before the counter again, alone, looking at another pot, almost the same colour as the one we saw. Looking at it, I feel like crying. I don't know why. Now I realize suddenly, it's because all that has gone.

When Fu had just got to know you, I remember once he came to our room and recited a line by Pushkin, "All that has happened in the past becomes a sweet memory." I pursed my lips and said it wasn't true. I even asked, "Can past misfortunes become sweet memories?" Fu grinned, ignoring me. He must have thought inwardly that I knew nothing about poetry. But today I understand. Pushkin was right. It exactly reflects my mood now. It's as if he wrote the line for me! I really feel that all the past is sweet.

A jet has just taken off, its engines roaring. Where is it going? In an hour, I'll be climbing up the steps into the plane, leaving my country. With only sixty minutes to go, I can't help weeping, and my tears wet this letter. But I've no time to re-write it.

I'm so depressed, I suddenly feel as if I've made the wrong decision. I don't want to leave everything here. No! I can't bear to leave our hospital, our operating theatre, even that little desk in the clinic! I often grumbled that Dr Sun was too severe, never forgiving a mistake. But now I wish I could hear his criticism again. He was a strict teacher. If not for him, I wouldn't be so skilled!

The loudspeakers have just wished passengers bon voyage. Will mine be good? Thinking of boarding the plane in a moment, I feel lost. Where will I land? What lies in stores? My heart's in my boots. I'm scared! Yes, scared stiff! Will we get used to a strange country, which is so different from ours? How can my mind be at peace?

My husband's sitting in an armchair brooding. Busy packing the last few days, he had no time to think. He seemed quite firm about the decision. But last night, when he stuffed the last coat into the suitcase, he said all of a sudden, "We'll be homeless from tomorrow!" He's not spoken since then, and I know his mind is still divided.

Yaya was most happy about this trip. She was nervous and excited, and sometimes I felt like hitting her. But now she's standing at the glass door watching the planes landing and taking off, as if reluctant to leave.

"Won't you change your minds?" you asked that night when we were at your place.

I can't answer that question in one sentence. Liu and I have been discussing it almost every day for the past few months. Our minds have been in a turmoil. There are many reasons, of course, urging us to leave China. It is for Yaya, for Liu and myself. However, none of those reasons can lessen my pain. We shouldn't leave, when China has just begun a new period. We've no excuse for avoiding our duties.

Compared with you, I'm a weaker character.

Though I had less trouble than you in the past ten years. I couldn't bear it as you did. I often burst out when viciously slandered and attacked. I wasn't stronger than you. On the contrary, it shows my weakness. Better to die than be humiliated, I thought. But there was Yaya. It was surprising that I was able to brazen it out in those days, when Liu was illegally detained as an "enemy agent".

All these are bitter memories of the past. Fu was right in saying, "Darkness has receded, and day has dawned." The trouble is, the evil influence of many years can't be eradicated overnight. The policies of the government take a long time to reach the people. Resentment is not easily removed. Rumours can kill a person. I dread such a nightmare. I lack your courage!

I remember that you and I were cited at that meeting as bourgeois specialists. When we left the hospital afterwards, I said to you, "I can't understand all this. Why should people who have worked hard in their field be crushed? I'll refuse to attend such meetings as a protest!" But you said, "Forget it! If they want to hold a hundred such meetings, let them. I'll attend. We'll still have to do the operations. I'll study at home." I asked you, "Don't you feel wronged?" You smiled and said, "I'm so busy, I've no time to care." I admired you very much. Before we parted, you warned me, "Don't tell Fu about such things. He's in enough trouble himself." We walked a block in silence. I noticed that you looked very calm, very confident. No one could shake your faith. I knew that you had a strong will, which enabled you to resist all kinds of attacks and go your own way. If I had half your courage and will-power, I wouldn't have made such a decision.

Forgive me! This is all I can say to you now. I'm leaving, but I'm leaving my heart with you, with my dear homeland. Wherever I go, I'll never forget China. Believe me! Believe that I'll return. After a few years, when Yaya's grown up and we have achieved something in medicine, we'll come back.

I hope you'll soon recover! Learn a lesson from your illness and pay more attention to your health. I'm not advising you to be selfish. I've always admired your selflessness. I wish you good health to make full use of your talents!

Goodbye, my dearest friend!

Affectionately,
Yafen

22

A month and a half later, Dr Lu had basically recovered and was permitted to go home.

It was a miracle. Ill as she was, Lu, several times on the brink of death, survived. The doctors were greatly surprised and delighted.

That morning, Fu jubilantly helped her put on a cotton-padded jacket, a pair of woollen trousers, a blue overcoat, and wrapped around her neck a long fluffy beige scarf.

"How are things at home?" she asked.

"Fine. The comrades of your Party branch came yesterday to help clean the room."

Her thoughts immediately turned to that small room with the large bookcase covered with a white cloth, the little alarm-clock on the window-sill and the desk. . . .

She felt feeble and cold, though so warmly dressed. Her legs trembled when she stood up. With one hand gripping her husband's arm, the other touching the wall, she moved forward leaning heavily on Fu. Slowly, she walked out of the ward.

Zhao, Sun and her other colleagues followed her, watching her progress along the corridor towards the gate.

It had rained for a couple of days. A gust of wind sighed through the bare branches of the trees. The sunshine, extraordinarily bright after the rain, slanted in through the windows of the corridor. The cold wind blew in too. Slowly Fu, supporting his wife, headed for the sunlight and the wind.

A black car was waiting at the steps. It had been sent by the administration department at Zhao's request.

Leaning on her husband's shoulder, Lu walked slowly towards the gate. . . .

Translated by Yu Fanqin and Wang Mingjie

Zhang Jie in 1980

Zhang Jie

Zhang Jie

ZHANG Jie, born in 1937, was the daughter of a teacher in Beijing. Having studied economics in the People's University, she was assigned to one of the industrial ministries. Later she transferred to the Beijing Film Studio and wrote the film scripts *The Search* and *We Are Still Young*. In 1978 her story "The Music of the Forests" won a prize as one of the best short stories of that year. She writes in a fresh, romantic style. Her "Love Must Not Be Forgotten" is a widely read and controversial story written in 1979. *Leaden Wings*, a longer and more ambitious story published in 1981, deals with some of the key problems in industry, different attitudes towards the modernization programme, and the involved relationships between a wide range of convincing characters. A member of the Chinese Writers' Association, Zhang Jie now works for the Beijing branch of the China Federation of Literary and Art Circles.

Love Must Not Be Forgotten

Zhang Jie

I am thirty, the same age as our People's Republic. For a republic thirty is still young. But a girl of thirty is virtually on the shelf.

Actually, I have a bona fide suitor. Have you seen the Greek sculptor Myron's Discobolus? Qiao Lin is the image of that discus thrower. Even the padded clothes he wears in winter fail to hide his fine physique. Bronzed, with clear-cut features, a broad forehead and large eyes, his appearance alone attracts most girls to him.

But I can't make up my mind to marry him. I'm not clear what attracts me to him, or him to me.

I know people are gossipping behind my back, "Who does she think she is, to be so choosy?"

To them, I'm a nobody playing hard to get. They take offence at such preposterous behaviour.

Of course, I shouldn't be captious. In a society where commercial production still exists, marriage like most other transactions is still a form of barter.

I have known Qiao Lin for nearly two years, yet still cannot fathom whether he keeps so quiet from aversion to talking or from having nothing to say. When, by way of a small intelligence test, I demand his opinion of this or that, he says "good" or "bad" like a child in kindergarten.

Once I asked, "Qiao Lin, why do you love me?" He thought the question over seriously for what seemed an age. I could see from his normally smooth but now wrinkled forehead that the little grey cells in his handsome head were hard at work cogitating. I felt ashamed to have put him on the spot.

Finally he raised his clear childlike eyes to tell me, "Because you're good!"

Loneliness flooded my heart. "Thank you, Qiao Lin!" I couldn't help wondering, if we were to marry, whether we could discharge our duties to each other as husband and wife. Maybe, because law and morality would have bound us together. But how tragic simply to comply with law and morality! Was there no stronger bond to link us?

When such thoughts cross my mind I have the strange sensation that instead of being a girl contemplating marriage I am an elderly social scientist.

Perhaps I worry too much. We can live like most married couples, bringing up children together, strictly true to each other according to the law. . . . Although living in the seventies of the twentieth century, people still consider marriage the way they did millennia ago, as a means of continuing the race, a form of barter or a business transaction in which love and marriage can be separated. As this is the common practice, why shouldn't we follow suit?

But I still can't make up my mind. As a child, I remember, I often cried all night for no rhyme or reason, unable to sleep and disturbing the whole household. My old nurse, a shrewd though uneducated woman, said an ill wind had blown through my ear. I think this judgement showed prescience, because I still have that old weakness. I upset myself over things which really present no problem, upsetting other people at the same time. One's nature is hard to change.

I think of my mother too. If she were alive, what would she say about my attitude to Qiao Lin and my uncertainty about marrying him?

My thoughts constantly turn to her, not because she was such a strict mother that her ghost is still watching over me since her death. No, she was not just my mother but my closest friend. I loved her so much that the thought of her leaving me makes my heart ache.

She never lectured me, just told me quietly in her deep, unwomanly voice about her successes and failures, so that I could learn from her experience. She had evidently not had many successes — her life was full of failures.

During her last days she followed me with her fine, expressive eyes, as if wondering how I would manage on my own and as if she had some important advice for me but hesitated to give it. She must have been worried by my naiveté and sloppy ways. She suddenly blurted out, "Shanshan, if you aren't sure what you want, don't rush into marriage — better live on your own!"

Other people might think this strange advice from a mother to her daughter, but to me it embodied her bitter experience. I don't think she underestimated me or my knowledge of life. She loved me and didn't want me to be unhappy.

"I don't want to marry, mum!" I said, not out of bashfulness or a show of coyness. I can't think why a girl should pretend to be coy. She had long since taught me about things not generally mentioned to girls.

"If you meet the right man, then marry him. Only if he's right for you!"

"I'm afraid no such man exists!"

"That's not true. But it's hard. The world is so vast, I'm afraid you may never meet him." Whether I married or not was not what concerned her, but the quality of the marriage.

"Haven't you managed fine without a husband?"

"Who says so?"

"I think you've done fine."

"I had no choice. . . ." She broke off, lost in thought, her face wistful. Her wistful lined face reminded me of a withered flower I had pressed in a book.

"Why did you have no choice?"

"You ask too many questions," she parried, not ashamed to confide in me but afraid that I might reach the wrong conclusion. Besides, everyone treasures a secret to carry to the grave. Feeling a bit put out, I demanded bluntly, "Didn't you love my dad?"

"No, I never loved him."

"Did he love you?"

"No, he didn't."

"Then why get married?"

She paused, searching for the right words to explain this mystery, then answered bitterly, "When you're young you don't always know what you're looking for, what you need, and people may talk you into getting married. As you grow older and more experienced you find out your true needs. By then, though, you've done many foolish things for which you could kick yourself. You'd give anything to be able to make a fresh start and live more wisely. Those content with their lot will always be happy, they say, but I shall never enjoy that happiness." She added self-mockingly, "A wretched idealist, that's all I am."

Did I take after her? Did we both have genes which attracted ill winds?

"Why don't you marry again?"

"I'm afraid I'm still not sure what I really want." She was obviously unwilling to tell me the truth.

I cannot remember my father. He and Mother split up when I was very small. I just recall her telling me sheepishly that he was a fine handsome fellow. I could see she was ashamed of having judged by appearances and made a futile choice. She told me, "When I can't sleep at night, I force myself to sober up by recalling all those stupid blunders I made. Of course it's so distasteful that I often hide my face in the sheet for shame, as if there were eyes watching me in the dark. But distasteful as it is, I take some pleasure in this form of atonement."

I was really sorry that she hadn't remarried. She was such a fascinating character, if she'd married a man she loved, what a happy household ours would surely have been. Though not beautiful, she had the simple charm of an ink landscape. She was a fine writer too. Another author who knew her well used to say teasingly, "Just reading your works is enough to make anyone love you!"

She would retort, "If he knew that the object of his affection was a white-haired old crone, that would frighten him away."

At her age, she must have known what she really

wanted, so this was obviously an evasion. I say this because she had quirks which puzzled me.

For instance, whenever she left Beijing on a trip, she always took with her one of the twenty-seven volumes of Chekov's stories published between 1950 and 1955. She also warned me, "Don't touch these books. If you want to read Chekov, read that set I bought you." There was no need to caution me. Having a set of my own why should I touch hers? Besides, she'd told me this over and over again. Still she was on her guard. She seemed bewitched by those books.

So we had two sets of Chekov's stories at home. Not just because we loved Chekov, but to parry other people like me who loved Chekov. Whenever anyone asked to borrow a volume, she would lend one of mine. Once, in her absence, a close friend took a volume from her set. When she found out she was frantic, and at once took a volume of mine to exchange for it.

Ever since I can remember, those books were on her bookcase. Although I admire Chekov as a great writer, I was puzzled by the way she never tired of reading him. Why, for over twenty years, had she had to read him every single day?

Sometimes, when tired of writing, she poured herself a cup of strong tea and sat down in front of the bookcase, staring raptly at that set of books. If I went into her room then it flustered her, and she either spilt her tea or blushed like a girl discovered with her lover.

I wondered: Has she fallen in love with Chekov? She might have if he'd still been alive.

When her mind was wandering just before her death, her last words to me were: "That set. . . ." She hadn't the strength to give it its complete title. But I knew what she meant. "And my diary. . . . 'Love Must Not Be Forgotten'. . . . Cremate them with me."

I carried out her last instruction regarding the works of Chekov, but couldn't bring myself to destroy her diary. I thought, if it could be published, it would surely prove the most moving thing she had written. But naturally publication was out of the question.

At first I imagined the entries were raw material she had jotted down. They read neither like stories, essays, a diary or letters. But after reading the whole I formed a hazy impression, helped out by my imperfect memory. Thinking it over, I finally realized that this was no life-less manuscript I was holding, but an anguished, loving heart. For over twenty years one man had occupied her heart, but he was not for her. She used these diaries as a substitute for him, a means of pouring out her feelings to him, day after day, year after year.

No wonder she had never considered any eligible pro-posals, had turned a deaf ear to idle talk whether well-meant or malicious. Her heart was already full, to the exclusion of anybody else. "No lake can compare with the ocean, no cloud with those on Mount Wu." Remem-bering those lines I often reflected sadly that few people in real life could love like this. No one would love me like this.

I learned that towards the end of the thirties, when this man was doing underground work for the Party in Shanghai, an old worker had given his life to cover him, leaving behind a helpless wife and daughter. Out of a sense of duty, of gratitude to the dead and deep class feeling, he had unhesitatingly married the girl. When he saw the endless troubles caused by "love" of couples who had married for "love", he may have thought,

"Thank Heaven, though I didn't marry for love, we get on well, able to help each other." For years, as man and wife they lived through hard times.

He must have been my mother's colleague. Had I ever met him? He couldn't have visited our home. Who was he?

In the spring of 1962, Mother took me to a concert. We went on foot, the theatre being quite near.

A black limousine pulled up silently by the pavement. Out stepped an elderly man with white hair in a black serge tunic-suit. What a striking shock of white hair! Strict, scrupulous, distinguished, transparently honest — that was my impression of him. The cold glint of his flashing eyes reminded me of lightning or swordplay. Only ardent love for a woman really deserving his love could fill cold eyes like those with tenderness.

He walked up to Mother and said, "How are you, Comrade Zhong Yu? It's been a long time."

"How are you!" Mother's hand holding mine suddenly turned icy cold and trembled a little.

They stood face to face without looking at each other, each appearing upset, even stern. Mother fixed her eyes on the trees by the roadside, not yet in leaf. He looked at me. "Such a big girl already. Good, fine — you take after your mother."

Instead of shaking hands with Mother he shook hands with me. His hand was as icy as hers and trembling a little. As if transmitting an electric current, I felt a sudden shock. Snatching my hand away I cried, "There's nothing good about that!"

"Why not?" he asked with the surprised expression grown-ups always have when children speak out frankly.

I glanced at Mother's face. I did take after her, to my disappointment. "Because she's not beautiful!"

He laughed, then said teasingly, "Too bad that there should be a child who doesn't find her own mother beautiful. Do you remember in '53, when your mum was transferred to Beijing, she came to our ministry to report for duty? She left you outside on the verandah, but like a monkey you climbed all the stairs, peeped through the cracks in doors, and caught your finger in the door of my office. You sobbed so bitterly that I carried you off to find her."

"I don't remember that." I was annoyed at his harking back to a time when I was still in open-seat pants.

"Ah, we old people have better memories." He turned abruptly and remarked to Mother, "I've read that last story of yours. Frankly speaking, there's something not quite right about it. You shouldn't have condemned the heroine.... There's nothing wrong with falling in love, as long as you don't spoil someone else's life.... In fact, the hero might have loved her too. Only for the sake of a third person's happiness, they had to renounce their love...."

A policeman came over to where the car was parked and ordered the driver to move on. When the driver made some excuse, the old man looked round. After a hasty "Goodbye" he strode to the car and told the policeman, "Sorry. It's not his fault, it's mine...."

I found it amusing watching this old cadre listening respectfully to the policeman's strictures. When I turned to Mother with a mischievous smile, she looked as upset as a first-form primary schoolchild standing forlornly in front of the stern headmistress. Anyone would have thought she was the one being lectured by the policeman.

The car drove off, leaving a puff of smoke. Very soon even this smoke vanished with the wind, as if nothing at all had happened. But the incident stuck in my mind.

Analysing it now, he must have been the man whose strength of character won Mother's heart. That strength came from his firm political convictions, his narrow escapes from death in the revolution, his active brain, his drive at work, his well-cultivated mind. Besides, strange to say, he and Mother both liked the oboe. Yes, she must have worshipped him. She once told me that unless she worshipped a man, she couldn't love him even for one day.

But I could not tell whether he loved her or not. If not, why was there this entry in her diary?

> "This is far too fine a present. But how did you know that Chekov's my favourite writer?"
> "You said so."
> "I don't remember that."
> "I remember. I heard you mention it when you were chatting with someone."

So he was the one who had given her the *Selected Stories of Chekov*. For her that was tantamount to a love letter.

Maybe this man, who didn't believe in love, realized by the time his hair was white that in his heart was something which could be called love. By the time he no longer had the right to love, he made the tragic discovery of this love for which he would have given his life. Or did it go deeper than that?

This is all I remember about him.

How wretched Mother must have been, deprived of the man to whom she was devoted! To catch a glimpse of his car or the back of his head through its rear window, she carefully figured out which roads he would take to work and back. Whenever he made a speech, she sat at the back of the hall watching his face rendered hazy by cigarette smoke and poor lighting. Her eyes would brim with tears, but she swallowed them back. If a fit of coughing made him break off, she wondered anxiously why no one persuaded him to give up smoking. She was afraid he would get bronchitis again. Why was he so near yet so far?

He, to catch a glimpse of her, looked out of the car window every day, straining his eyes to watch the streams of cyclists, afraid that she might have an accident. On the rare evenings on which he had no meetings, he would walk by a roundabout way to our neighbourhood, to pass our compound gate. However busy, he would always make time to look in papers and journals for her work.

His duty had always been clear to him, even in the most difficult times. But now confronted by this love he became a weakling, quite helpless. At his age it was laughable. Why should life play this trick on him?

Yet when they happened to meet at work, each tried to avoid the other, hurrying off with a nod. Even so, this would make Mother blind and deaf to everything around her. If she met a colleague named Wang she would call him Guo and mutter something unintelligible.

It was a cruel ordeal for her. She wrote:

We agreed to forget each other. But I deceived

you, I have never forgotten. I don't think you've forgotten either. We're just deceiving each other, hiding our misery. I haven't deceived you deliberately, though; I did my best to carry out our agreement. I often stay far away from Beijing, hoping time and distance will help me to forget you. But on my return, as the train pulls into the station, my head reels. I stand on the platform looking round intently, as if someone were waiting for me. Of course there is no one. I realize then that I have forgotten nothing. Everything is unchanged. My love is like a tree the roots of which strike deeper year after year — I have no way to uproot it.

At the end of every day, I feel as if I've forgotten something important. I may wake with a start from my dreams wondering what has happened. But nothing has happened. Nothing. Then it comes home to me that you are missing! So everything seems lacking, incomplete, and there is nothing to fill up the blank. We are nearing the ends of our lives, why should we be carried away by emotion like children? Why should life submit people to such ordeals, then unfold before you your lifelong dream? Because I started off blindly I took the wrong turning, and now there are insuperable obstacles between me and my dream.

Yes, Mother never let me go to the station to meet her when she came back from a trip, preferring to stand alone on the platform and imagine that he had met her. Poor mother with her greying hair was as infatuated as a girl.

Not much space in the diary was devoted to their romance. Most entries dealt with trivia: Why one of her articles had not come off; her fear that she had no real talent; the excellent play she missed by mistaking the time on the ticket; the drenching she got by going out for a stroll without her umbrella. In spirit they were together day and night, like a devoted married couple. In fact, they spent no more than twenty-four hours together in all. Yet in that time they experienced deeper happiness than some people in a whole lifetime. Shakespeare makes Juliet say, "I cannot sum up half my sum of wealth." And probably that is how Mother felt.

He must have been killed in the "cultural revolution". Perhaps because of the conditions then, that section of the diary is ambiguous and obscure. Mother had been so fiercely attacked for her writing, it amazed me that she went on keeping a diary. From some veiled allusions I gathered that he had queried the theories advanced by that "theoretician" then at the height of favour, and had told someone, "This is sheer Rightist talk." It was clear from the tear-stained pages of Mother's diary that he had been harshly denounced; but the steadfast old man never knuckled under to the authorities. His last words were, "When I go to meet Marx, I shall go on fighting my case!"

That must have been in the winter of 1969, because that was when Mother's hair turned white overnight, though she was not yet fifty. And she put on a black arm-band. Her position then was extremely difficult. She was criticized for wearing this old-style mourning, and ordered to say for whom she was in mourning.

"For whom are you wearing that, mum?" I asked anxiously.

"For my lover." Not to frighten me she explained, "Someone you never knew."

"Shall I put one on too?" She patted my cheeks, as she had when I was a child. It was years since she had shown me such affection. I often felt that as she aged, especially during these last years of persecution, all tenderness had left her, or was concealed in her heart, so that she seemed like a man.

She smiled sadly and said, "No, you needn't wear one."

Her eyes were as dry as if she had no more tears to shed. I longed to comfort her or do something to please her. But she said, "Off you go."

I felt an inexplicable dread, as if dear Mother had already half left me. I blurted out, "Mum!"

Quick to sense my desolation, she said gently, "Don't be afraid. Off you go. Leave me alone for a little."

I was right. She wrote:

You have gone. Half my soul seems to have taken flight with you.

I had no means of knowing what had become of you, much less of seeing you for the last time. I had no right to ask either, not being your wife or friend. ... So we are torn apart. If only I could have borne that inhuman treatment for you, so that you could have lived on! You should have lived to see your name cleared and take up your work again, for the sake of those who loved you. I knew you could not be a counter-revolutionary. You were one of the finest men killed. That's why I love you — I am not afraid now to avow it.

Snow is whirling down. Heavens, even God is

such a hypocrite, he is using this whiteness to cover up your blood and the scandal of your murder.

I have never set store by my life. But now I keep wondering whether anything I say or do would make you contract your shaggy eyebrows in a frown. I must live a worthwhile life like you, and do some honest work for our country. Things can't go on like this — those criminals will get what's coming to them.

I used to walk alone along that small asphalt road, the only place where we once walked together, hearing my footsteps in the silent night. . . . I always paced to and fro and lingered there, but never as wretchedly as now. Then, though you were not beside me, I knew you were still in this world and felt that you were keeping me company. Now I can hardly believe that you have gone.

At the end of the road I would retrace my steps, then walk along it again.

Rounding the fence I always looked back, as if you were still standing there waving goodbye. We smiled faintly, like casual acquaintances, to conceal our undying love. That ordinary evening in early spring, a chilly wind was blowing as we walked silently away from each other. You were wheezing a little because of your chronic bronchitis. That upset me. I wanted to beg you to slow down, but somehow I couldn't. We both walked very fast, as if some important business were waiting for us. How we prized that single stroll we had together, but we were afraid we might lose control of ourselves and burst out with "I love you" — those three words which had tormented us for years.

Probably no one else could believe that we never once even clasped hands!

No, Mother, I believe it. I am the only one able to see into your locked heart.

Ah, that little asphalt road, so haunted by bitter memories. We shouldn't overlook the most insignificant spots on earth. For who knows how much secret grief and joy they may hide.

No wonder that when tired of writing, she would pace slowly along that little road behind our window. Sometimes at dawn after a sleepless night, sometimes on a moonless, windy evening. Even in winter during howling gales which hurled sand and pebbles against the window pace. . . . I thought this was one of her eccentricities, not knowing that she had gone to meet him in spirit.

She liked to stand by the window too, staring at the small asphalt road. Once I thought from her expression that one of our closest friends must be coming to call. I hurried to the window. It was a late autumn evening. The cold wind was stripping dead leaves from the trees and blowing them down the small empty road.

She went on pouring out her heart to him in her diary as she had when he was alive. Right up to the day when the pen slipped from her fingers. Her last message was:

> I am a materialist, yet I wish there were a Heaven. For then, I know, I would find you there waiting for me. I am going there to join you, to be together for eternity. We need never be parted again or keep at a distance for fear of spoiling

someone else's life. Wait for me, dearest, I am coming —

I do not know how Mother, on her death bed, could still love so ardently with all her heart. To me it seemed not love but a form of madness, a passion stronger than death. If undying love really exists, she reached its extreme. She obviously died happy, because she had known true love. She had no regrets.

Now these old people's ashes have mingled with the elements. But I know that, no matter what form they may take, they still love each other. Though not bound together by earthly laws or morality, though they never once clasped hands, each possessed the other completely. Nothing could part them. Centuries to come, if one white cloud trails another, two grasses grow side by side, one wave splashes another, a breeze follows another... believe me, that will be them.

Each time I read that diary "Love Must Not Be Forgotten" I cannot hold back my tears. I often weep bitterly, as if I myself experienced their ill-fated love. If not a tragedy it was too laughable. No matter how beautiful or moving I find it, I have no wish to follow suit!

Thomas Hardy wrote that "the call seldom produces the comer, the man to love rarely coincides with the hour for loving". I cannot censure them from conventional moral standards. What I deplore is that they did not wait for a "missing counterpart" to call them.

If everyone could wait, instead of rushing into marriage, how many tragedies could be averted!

When we reach communism, will there still be cases of marriage without love? Maybe, because since the world is so vast, two kindred spirits may be unable to answer each other's call. But how tragic! However, by that time, there may be ways to escape such tragedies.

Why should I split hairs?

Perhaps after all we are responsible for these tragedies. Who knows? Maybe we should take the responsibility for the old ideas handed down from the past. Because if someone never marries, that is a challenge to these ideas. You will be called neurotic, accused of having guilty secrets or having made political mistakes. You may be regarded as an eccentric who looks down on ordinary people, not respecting age-old customs — a heretic. In short they will trump up endless vulgar and futile charges to ruin your reputation. Then you have to knuckle under to those ideas and marry willy-nilly. But once you put the chains of a loveless marriage around your neck, you will suffer for it for the rest of your life.

I long to shout: "Mind your own business! Let us wait patiently for our counterparts. Even waiting in vain is better than willy-nilly marriage. To live single is not such a fearful disaster. I believe it may be a sign of a step forward in culture, education and the quality of life."

Translated by Gladys Yang

Zhang Kangkang in 1980

Zhang Kangkang

ZHANG Kangkang, born in 1950, writes from first hand experience about young people's problems. She first became known for her story "The Right to Love". Still at the start of her literary career she is a professional writer, a member of the Chinese Writers' Association.

The Wasted Years

Zhang Kangkang

LATE at night something was knocked over in the dark, narrow corridor. A commotion broke the silence, followed by the thud of footsteps. When they reached my door they stopped.

Bang! Bang! Someone hammered on my door.

Putting down my pen I stood up and glanced at the alarm-clock on my desk — it was a quarter to eleven. At that hour only hard-working, impatient students would come to these staff quarters.

"I'm looking for Mr Peng! Does he live here?" a male voice gasped.

"That's me. Please come in," I called out.

With a gust of cold late autumn air, they entered my room. Two strangers, simply dressed, a middle-aged couple, they stood warily in the centre of my room. I felt there was something unusual about the swollen eyes of the woman and the sullen expression of the man.

"Do you know Xu Li?" the man asked, after a short silence.

"He's a boy!" The woman added and wiped the corner of her eyes with her dirty scarf.

"Xu Li? Sorry, I don't know him," I answered, shaking my head.

"Didn't he come here?" the man asked incredulously, coughing.

I had nothing to say, only shook my head once more.

The woman suddenly covered her face with her scarf, crying out, "If he's not been here, where could he be?"

"What's the matter? What's happened? Please keep calm and tell me what it's all about."

"What's happened!? Don't you know? You taught him and drove him crazy! He can't be compared to you. You're a teacher and he's a fool who knows nothing!" The man glared at me furiously. His outburst puzzled me.

"Xu Li?" I dug into my memory for the name. The eyebrows of the angry man and the wide mouth of the woman, who was weeping, reminded me vaguely of someone. I asked myself, "Who's Xu Li?" The name seemed somewhat familiar.

"Isn't this the note you wrote to him? Look. . . ." He took out a crumpled sheet of paper from his pocket and handed it to me.

"Did you write this to him? You wasted your time. He's an idiot. . . ."

I recognized my own handwriting: "Comrade Xu Li. . . ." Immediately I recalled a shy young man with the same broad eyebrows as his father, the same wide mouth as his mother. I was astonished and worried.

". . . Please let him come home. . . ." The mother was crying. "Oh! My second son. . . . Why did you run away from home. . . ?"

It was late at night. The noise would disturb my neighbours. I begged her to keep calm, explaining that I had known Xu Li only briefly. He had once come to see me to borrow a book. My note was to inform him that I had got it for him. That was all I knew.

"I had no idea he'd run away from home," I said, feeling very sorry for them.

They looked at each other and gazed around the room, as if to check that such a small room, only fourteen square metres, could not conceal their missing son. They had nothing more to say, but the mother muttered with bent head, "He's been gone for three days...."

"Why did he run away from home?" I could not suppress my curiosity.

"Who knows? Humph! No note, just disappeared. ..." The father shook his head desperately.

"Could it be...?" I ventured cautiously. "Such.... Does he have a girlfriend? Or like...."

His mother cut in, "He blushes at the very sight of a girl and seldom goes out. He likes reading all day and always works hard. Everyone praises my second son.... Ah, son, even though your father lost his temper and hit you, you shouldn't have run away...."

It was obvious that they could not explain the matter, and I knew nothing about their family quarrels. I was concerned not only for the boy but also for his parents, who could not account for their son's disappearance. Perhaps they didn't want me to know the real truth.

"Look," I glanced at the clock, saying, "since Xu Li asked me to borrow a book for him, he'll probably come to collect it. When he comes, I'll notify you of his whereabouts as quickly as possible. OK?"

After thinking this over for a moment, they agreed and looked more kindly at me. The mother even murmured something like, "Sorry to trouble you...." As I walked them to the door, the father gave me their address, trying to describe the place clumsily with his big hands. I guessed he was a carpenter in a factory.

"Don't borrow books for Xu Li next time, if he asks you. The boy's an idiot. What's the use of reading history? You, as a teacher, shouldn't waste your time on the boy," the father advised me, frowning.

Confused and dazed, I forgot to see them off.

More noise, then the footsteps faded and the building lapsed into silence once again.

I made some strong tea for myself and sat down.

Strictly speaking, I'd met Xu Li only once, fifteen days ago. I hadn't thought of him as my student, though I was ten years older and he actually had asked me to be his teacher. I hardly knew him, yet took to him at once.

That day after class someone followed me downstairs. When I reached the door of the staff-room, he came up to me and shyly asked, "Excuse me, are you Mr Peng?"

"Yes, what do you want?" I stopped at the door, examining him: a thin young man, whose appearance made a good impression on me.

"I. . . ." He stammered and blushed a little, "I just read your article on the development of contemporary capitalism published in the magazine. I'd like to. . . ."

I was always being pounced on by people interested in discussing academic problems with me. Not wanting to embarrass him I suggested, "Look, I'm sorry. I've still another two classes to teach. Please come to see me next Sunday. I'm in the fifth block, second flat, third floor."

He wanted to add something, but hesitated. Swallowing the words, he nodded and left.

Sunday afternoon he did come, lightly tapping my unlocked door, suddenly appearing before me.

"Please sit down!" I beckoned to him.

"Oh! No...." He stood in the middle of my room, staring at his feet and shivered.

I suddenly saw his drenched clothes and hair wet with rain. Hurriedly I took a towel and passed it to him, asking, "Is it pelting?"

"Yes."

"Why didn't you bring an umbrella?"

"... Umbrella? I can't use one at work...."

"Work? What work?"

"I shovel stones and load them on trucks. The work-site's not far from here. I've worked there for several months. But, only recently I found out your address."

"You're a...?"

"I'm waiting for a permanent job. Being a navvy is only temporary. It was lucky it rained today, or I wouldn't have been able to visit you." He seemed a pleasant young fellow.

"Waiting for a job?" I was surprised. Why should he want to see me, a teacher of history? I gave him some dry clothes to change into. Suddenly he produced a small book from his jacket pocket. The plastic cover had got wet at the edges. He carefully placed it on the desk, then changed his clothes.

It was well-thumbed Xinhua Chinese dictionary. He felt embarrassed when I looked at it. Then he smiled awkwardly. "The classics are quite difficult to read. There are many sentences I can't understand...." He sat down and added, "But I can understand what you've written and your penetrating analyses. Some of your viewpoints are new and no one has ever explained them before."

"Such as?"

"When you said that capitalism developed from the

ancient Greeks and Romans, but it had been impossible for China, India and Russia to develop it completely, because capitalism is not only an economic phenomenon but also a cultural one. . . ."

I was interested in hearing this, because this young man had caught the main theme of the article, though not profoundly enough. It seemed he had really used his mind. My nodding encouraged him to speak more freely, and I realized that he had read many history books.

"In history, the loyal officials were always defeated by the treacherous ones at court," he said, pursing his mouth seriously. "That is because the former concentrated on being loyal, while the latter spent most of their energies on worsting the former. In the end, of course, the treacherous officials won. This is the conclusion I arrived at after reading history. Was this correct or not?"

Suddenly I felt drawn to him. Some of my students studied history only for their diploma; very few were really fond of it, but this young man was one of them. Teachers always love their subjects. History to me was like an encyclopaedia full of almost all the original sources for the events of every period. It was also like a steamboat going against the current. People can trace the causes and effects of the human comedies and tragedies of their times by studying history. On the other hand history is history, a pile of classical files, a science with no material benefits. Who would be interested in studying it? It was strange to find a young man like him reading history on his own initiative. What was going on in his mind? Belonging to two different generations, what chance had brought us together?

"Since you've read many books on history, are you preparing to study it at university?" I asked.

He was so puzzled by my remark that he could hardly speak. "Oh, no," he murmured. "I couldn't pass the entrance examination, my Chinese and foreign languages are too poor. Not me. I just returned here the year before last. I'm waiting for a permanent job."

"Where were you before?"

"Working in the countryside. I'd just started middle school when the 'cultural revolution' broke out, so I missed out on my basic grounding. . . ." His gaze seemed fixed on something within sight yet out of reach. Heaving a deep sigh he said, "University. . . . I've no chance. I'm too ignorant. . . ."

His honesty saddened me. All around me were university students, today's élite. Did we ever stop to think of all the youngsters like him waiting for permanent jobs outside the campus?

I made some tea for him.

"You study by yourself?"

He nodded, saying, "Years ago a history teacher lent me some books. . . . Later he moved to another place. Then I tried to borrow books from other people. I can't really explain why I enjoy reading history. But I think history is like a mirror reflecting the truth. We understand many things better after studying it."

"You can come to our university and sit in on the course." My sympathy made me suggest this. "I can manage this for you, if you like."

On hearing this, his face brightened up and his eyes were full of excitement. But it faded away quickly.

"That's impossible. I have to work in the daytime,

thirty days a month. My parents don't allow me....
You might not know...."

He lowered his head, as if at a loss for words. After a pause, he continued hesitantly, "You don't know, but when I failed the university entrance examination, they wanted me to sell bean sprouts in the free market to earn six to seven yuan a day, but I refused. If I worked more than ten hours a day, I'd have no time to study. I prefer this navvy's job, though it brings in less money. After the trucks are loaded I have some time to study."

I thought of his dictionary.

"As a temporary worker I can't ask for leave. Each month I hand my wages over...."He broke off.

"So how do you study...?" I asked.

"After nine o'clock at night. I share a small room with my younger sister. I have a bed and a desk. After she finishes her homework I can use the desk and start studying. After nine o'clock the time is mine...." He smiled, as if he felt quite satisfied and fortunate. I could see he was proud of his half of the small room. Compared with his my room of fourteen square metres was paradise.

It was getting dark. I turned on the light.

"Oh!" He jumped to his feet, taking off my sweater and picking up his dictionary. "It's time for me to leave. I must get back and cook supper for my younger brother and sister while they do their homework."

He put on his wet clothes.

"Thank you very much, Mr Peng! You've been so kind. I'm sorry to waste your precious time, but I felt so lonely and bored."

His eyes glittered in the dark corridor.

"May I borrow a book from you?" he asked hesitantly.

"What book?"

"*On Evolution* translated by Yan Fu".

"*On Evolution*! Sorry, I don't have it, but I'll borrow it from the university library." I was surprised, because the book was an abridged summary of the first two chapters of *Evolution and Ethics* by T. H. Huxley. Could he really understand the contents? Suddenly I thought of lending him an umbrella. By the time I turned to get it, he had disappeared into the darkness.

It was still raining.

"My name's Xu Li!" His voice sounded in the distance in the rain.

Could Xu Li, this diffident, unusual young man, have run away from home? He showed such respect for his parents and such concern for his younger brother and sister, why should he have run away from them? I could not think of a reason. But after talking with him that night, I should have realized that he had something on his mind.

The tea was already cold, so I did not drink it. I would not sleep that night. I felt sure that he would come to see me again, because he wanted the book. I only hoped he had not got involved in any trouble.

The next day there was a meeting arranged by the provincial historical research society, so I did not get home until four in the afternoon. As I opened the door I found a scrap of white paper on the floor. On it was written:

Mr Peng,

    I came to see you to collect the book you promised to lend me, but you were out. I am not living at home now and I have a new job, a very nice one. My new address is the Logistics Team, 7381 Shelter Construction Headquarters. I'll tell you more about my situation when I see you.

His handwriting was badly formed, like that of most young people who had read widely but who lacked a good academic grounding. Still I was happy to know that he had a new job which he liked.

"7381" was a big construction project for air raid defence. Without much difficulty I found the headquarters, a row of simple huts roofed with corrugated iron and with small signboards. I entered the Logistics Team office and asked for Xu Li. A man looking like a cadre answered with a yawn, "Who's Xu Li? Never heard of him."

"Please check again. He's a new temporary worker."

"We're not in charge of temporary workers." He turned to answer a telephone call, ignoring me.

I left in a huff, wondering why they did not know of him. Xu Li had said he had found a very nice job. Why should he lie to me? Where could I find him?

I wandered with my bicycle about the worksite, hoping to find someone to ask. It was getting dark. I saw smoke rising from the chimney of a small wooden hut. Someone was busy at work. I went over and asked, "Comrade —"

He was bending down to pick something up. At the sound of my voice, he turned round. It was Xu Li!

"Xu Li!" I shouted.

He brightened up and his face broadened into a smile of astonishment. He could not believe that I had really come to see him. After a silence he began, "Mr Peng —"

"When I got your note I came here to give you the book," I told him casually. "And also to see what nice new job you've got!"

"Boiling water," he answered.

"Boiling water?"

"Yes, I boil the water in the boiler room." He put down the things he was carrying by the door of the hut, and pointed inside, saying, "That's my new home."

I ducked my head to enter and saw a wooden bed set up in a corner with a thin quilt on it and a locked wooden chest near it. The bed was covered with a sheet of cellophane. Opposite it was the boiler.

"Please, wait!" Wiping the cellophane clean with a rag, he apologized, "So much dust...."

I sat down on the bed. The lumpy mattress felt uncomfortable. Lifting it I saw many history magazines below.

With a shrug of his shoulders, Xu Li smiled. "Now I've more time to read. My job is to boil water, add coal and see to the fire. The night-shift workers drink less water. One boilerful is enough. So now I have more time to study. At the same time I needn't cook."

He seemed happy and contented. But as I looked around, the damp floor, low ceiling and dim light struck me as most depressing.

"Why did you shift here? Do you earn more?" I immediately felt that my questions were ridiculous.

"Compared with my last job I earn less," he answered.

"Why come here then?"

He lowered his head, gazing at his shoes and was

silent, his expression the same as when he had first come to my room.

"I. . . ." He stopped and rubbed his eyes with his rough hands. Then he went on in a husky voice, "I. . . I've no place to stay. . . ."

"Your family? Isn't there still a small room for you?"

Another silence, only the seething water in the boiler sounded like the young man sighing. The red glow from the fire could not cheer him up.

"Not any more. . . . My uncle's going to get married. Since he's no home, my father gave him the small room which can only hold a double-bed. I'd have to share a bed with my younger brother. I wouldn't be able to study late at night because the light disturbs my parents. . . ."

Suddenly he wept and choked out, ". . . To sell bean sprouts would earn more money. They told me to do it. With more money they said I could get a girlfriend. . . . I don't want to earn more money, so I refused to sell bean sprouts. But I had nowhere to study. . . . Then a classmate of mine helped me. His uncle, the former boiler man, gave up this job because it didn't pay well. But I don't mind. . . ."

Now I knew what had happened to him. No need for more explanations. The ten years of chaos had been a disaster for him, and in addition he had bigoted parents. Ordinarily he didn't even have a place to shed tears.

He stood up, raising one arm to wipe his face with his sleeve, then added one more shovel of coal to the furnace. The sparkling black coal blazed with a flame like blue satin.

"Mr Peng. . . ." His voice broke into my thoughts. He

had stopped weeping. Biting his lower lip, he suddenly spoke loudly, "Do you think I'm stupid and have no future at all?"

"Who says you're stupid? You can try again next year to get into university."

"If I fail again, will I have any future?" he asked. "I'm not studying so as to enter university or get a good job. I study history to broaden my understanding. I don't want to be an idiot. . . ." He was getting tired and worked up, leaning against the wooden wall.

The small room was roasting hot from the roaring fire.

I walked over and stood beside him, gently putting my hand on his head, intending to say: "Come to my place. I'll help you make up the lessons you've missed. I'm your friend. We can study together." But my throat was too constricted to speak. Young people still had ideals and valued their time, though it had been wasted during the ten chaotic years. . . . Now society was helping them fill up the gaps in their education. If parents and teachers were really concerned about them and tried in every possible way to help them, their deplorable situation should soon change.

He gave me a sesame seed cake and a green Chinese onion. I ate them with a bowl of hot water. It was delicious, and he seemed more animated.

We looked at each other, silent for a long time. Before I took my leave, he scratched his head and began, "Mr Peng, please don't tell anyone else that I'm here boiling water. Please promise. . . ?"

I suddenly remembered my promise to his parents. "I don't know any of your friends yet."

He spoke uneasily, "For example, my parents. I

haven't told them where I am. If they know, they'll force me back to sell bean sprouts. They oppose my studying and earning less money. But money can't buy time. Now I have more time to study. Once I get permanent work, I'll be very busy. Do you agree? Please don't tell my parents I'm here. When I get my monthly wage, after paying for my food and buying some books, I'll send the rest home." His eyes pleaded with me but I did not meet his gaze directly.

The door was open. The lamplight revealed that the black things piled before the door were lumps of poor quality coal.

"Oh!" He squatted on the ground, picking them up like precious stones and throwing them on to the heap of coal in the room. "It's a pity to throw them away," he said to himself. "They're not the best, but they can still be burnt."

I got on my bicycle and waved goodbye. Suddenly my front wheel bumped into a lump of coal and knocked it aside.

Turning my head, I saw Xu Li silhouetted against the light. On my way back, I was no longer worried about him. But should I tell his parents that he was here boiling water? What would be the outcome if they knew? I debated with myself but couldn't decide what to do.

Translated by Shen Zhen

Wang Anyi in 1980

Wang Anyi

WANG Anyi, born in Fujian in 1954, is the daughter of Ru Zhijuan. Not yet thirty, she represents the younger generation of writers whose formal education was disrupted by the "cultural revolution", and who were sent to the countryside to work. She knows from first-hand experience the problems of young people who have returned from communes to the cities. "Life in a Small Courtyard" describes young married couples living in crowded quarters on a small budget — except for the privileged son of a bureau director. Simply and honestly written, it tells us much about the quality of life in China today and the different senses of value of the writer's generation.

Wang Anyi has written several short stories and the long story "The Newly Arrived Coach". A member of the Chinese Writers' Association, she is an editor of the Shanghai magazine *Childhood*.

Life in a Small Courtyard

Wang Anyi

JUST as we returned from our tour, the new building of the Municipal Song and Dance Ensemble had at last been completed. Meanwhile, the houses in the old small courtyard near the East Railway Station, which had originally been our headquarters, were now to be used as accommodation for our families. Moreover, it was rumoured that the station square was to be enlarged and our small courtyard was just within the limit of those houses marked for demolition. It meant that in the near future the authorities would reallocate us new living quarters. The future looked good. Within a couple of days, the rehearsal hall, together with the small stage in the courtyard, had been divided into more than ten separate rooms; the building used for storing the sets was also divided into four rooms. Even the kitchen was transformed into two rooms. No reason to turn up your nose at our untidy small courtyard; it allowed some young couples to get married, and had also enabled a number of families of three generations crowded into a single room to separate. As a result, Aping and I were given a room in the former rehearsal hall. Though it was by no means large, neither was it too small. When the new living quarters were allocated we would be able to get a small flat. Before long, all the rooms in the courtyard, except an eight-square-metre room beside the lavatory, were occupied. Thus, the housing problem of the Municipal Song and Dance Ensemble was, at last, solved. Even more, the two sunniest and biggest office rooms, which could be exchanged later for a suite of three rooms and a kitchen, had been occupied by Huang Jian, the son of the director of the Cultural Bureau, and his wife Li Xiuwen, who were not members of our troupe.

Originally, these two rooms had been left vacant. Perhaps we all realized that such good rooms could not belong to us. Even if we had occupied them temporarily, we would sooner or later have had to move out. An inconvenience. Wiser to make a more modest choice from the very beginning. As was expected, a week later, Huang Jian and his wife moved into the two best rooms in our courtyard.

On the first night, Xiuwen forcibly dragged me to her home. I stopped dead in my tracks at the door, unable to recognize our old office room. From the centre of its light-blue ceiling hung a creamy chandelier. A suite of natural coloured wood-grain furniture appeared both simple and tasteful. A spring-mattressed bed was covered by a dark green and black rhombus-patterned counterpane. Over its head was a white wall light. Between a pair of small armchairs stood a floor lamp with an apple-green lampshade, casting a soft green circle of light on the floor. It was like a miracle.

The scene reminded me suddenly of the little room in which Xiuwen and I had lived together in the past. There four beds had been placed side by side. The one nearest the wall had a bed-spread made of hand-woven cloth and a rattan suitcase at the side. It was

Xiuwen's. Next to her was mine. We had just been transferred from the countryside with a wage of eighteen yuan per month.

And now, wearing a pair of red thick-soled slippers, Xiuwen gracefully paced up and down the light-green room. After turning on her large TV set, she handed me a cup of milk and a dish of cakes. She had become prettier, almost enchanting. Of course, she had always been attractive. At first, she was a member of our chorus. Later on, due to some problem with her voice, she could no longer sing. The ensemble kept her as an announcer. When she first stood before the microphone, the audience whispered, commenting on her appearance. Huang Jian was one of her ardent admirers. However, Huang Jian's first love had not been Xiuwen but. . . . How far my thoughts had drifted! I shook my head.

"Does the milk taste bad?" Xiuwen asked in amazement.

"Oh no, it's fine." I awkwardly tried to gloss over my blunder. "But, I don't really want it. I've just had supper."

"Then, have some fruit?" Picking up a big pear from the fruit tray, she peeled it slowly with a stainless knife and cut it into slices, which she stuck on some toothpicks. She handed them to me.

"Your room's lovely!" I exclaimed sincerely, full of praise. I reached for a second slice of pear. I was not used to this dainty way of eating fruit. In the past, I could have gobbled down several large pears at one go, when the ensemble distributed fruit bought cheaply from an orchard. Xiuwen could devour even more than I. Now she merely nibbled at a slice.

"Although Huang Jian isn't from Shanghai, he has

good taste. Whatever I like, he always tries his best to get it for me." Her smile was self-satisfied. "I haven't seen your place yet! Aping and you are both from Shanghai, so your home must be beautiful!"

"Some home! When we're on tour, our home goes with us."

"That's true. You should try to change your job. Do you want to be a dancer all your life?"

"Of course not. When I'm too old to dance, the troupe will find something else for me to do."

"Then it'll be too late. Look at me, I'm now working as a typist in the Cultural Bureau. It's an easy job. In fact, typists are badly needed in several other places too. Try to find some way to get transferred!"

"Easier said than done!" I sighed, reaching for my fourth slice of pear, and saying to myself, "Who can compare with you? The daughter-in-law of the bureau director."

Suddenly the window was pushed open with a bang, as three little heads and staring eyes emerged above the window-sill. Following their line of vision, I saw on television a fierce fight going on. Turning my head again, I recognized they were Jiang Mai's children. Having graduated from the Provincial Art College in 1967, Jiang Mai had joined us as a trombonist. Some said just after his graduation, Jiang Mai was a smart fellow, and there had been a number of young girls madly chasing after him. Carried away by this, he overdid things. His handsome looks quickly faded. All his girlfriends ditched him. When he was thirty, he finally found a young girl worker called Xiao Zhang, who agreed to marry him. Their domestic bliss was brief. Xiao Zhang insisted on having a daughter. But unfortunately, she gave birth to three sons in succession, and if our leader had not hinted enough is enough, she would surely have given birth to a fourth or fifth! Owing to their tight financial situation, the couple quarrelled and grumbled frequently. Though their neighbour for only a week, I was already accustomed to their constant bickering. You can't imagine how they sniped at one another!

Going over to the window, Xiuwen smiled at the three boys and invited them in. The children, however, were not used to such hospitality and shyly disappeared. I remembered how Xiuwen disliked being disturbed. On tour when some of our colleagues brought their children with them and the kids cried or made a noise at night, Xiuwen would complain bitterly. Now, she had changed completely. How a comfortable life can improve one's tolerance of others!

Huang Jian returned. On seeing me at first, he was slightly aghast but quickly recovered his composure and went to wash his hands. Why be like that? Let bygones be bygones. Ever since he became friendly with Xiuwen, I had left him alone. But it seemed, he still hated me. I often had a laugh over it. But now, I also felt somewhat uneasy. Before swallowing the last slice of pear, I stood up and hastily took my leave.

Passing a room which had originally been used as a dressing room, I heard someone saying, ". . . She's not pretty at all. Granted she has large eyes, yet they're expressionless. She has a high nose, but it's a snub one." The speaker was Ren Jia, wife of Hai Ping. She was well-known for her jealousy. Ren Jia was afraid her husband was too handsome and she was too plain. It made her very nervous, and that, in turn, made all of us very nervous too. One of her methods was to attack other girls. At this moment, I didn't know whom she was going on about. Xiuwen's eyes were both large and beautiful. As for me, people said that my nose was high, but only Aping considered that it was a bit retroussé. Was Ren Jia speaking about Xiuwen or me?

As I entered my "home", I saw Aping practising conducting ecstatically before a mirror. He used to talk a lot about music and poetry before our marriage. How had I been fascinated by such unworldly things!

2

The next morning, I saw Xiao Ji, a carpenter with the stage design group, squatting at the entrance of the lavatory and brushing his teeth. I was puzzled. It took me three or four minutes to make it out. He must have moved into the small eight-square-metre room. Its door formed a right angle with that of the lavatory. But I had still no idea when he had moved in there. He hadn't made any noise. The stage design group of our ensemble was, as a matter of fact, regarded as the most unimportant section, and its carpenters were practically anonymous. Furthermore, Xiao Ji was, by nature, a simple, taciturn man. Nobody ever took any notice of him.

We were having breakfast when Xiao Ji stepped into our room. As he was a rare visitor, we stood up to welcome him. Smiling shyly, he handed us two packets of sweets. Waving his hand, Aping said, "No need for that!" Xiao Ji's face turned red. I realized what they meant and immediately took them, saying, "Congratulations!" Xiao Ji turned and left, while Aping was still saying, "No need for that!" What an ass! Only after I had held them up for several minutes so that he could read the "wedding sweets" printed on them, did he exclaim, "Oh! He's got married!"

"You're so thick!" I scolded.

This irritated him, so he explained, "The change was too sudden. I wasn't prepared for it."

I ignored him, but thought to myself that there was some truth in what he said. We were not prepared at all. There had not been the slightest warning. Xiao Ji always did things quietly. But, who was his bride?

Having finished our meal, we locked our door and went to fetch our bikes. Jiang Mai, Hai Ping and his wife also got theirs. We all glanced simultaneously at Xiao Ji's room. He was just locking the door. Beside him stood a young girl dressed in a purple jacket, with a dark grey scarf round her neck. Her plaits were coiled up on top of her head. Her forehead and mouth were both very broad. She wore a pair of spectacles. They came over to us. Xiao Ji gave a nervous smile but the girl was relaxed and accepted our curious glances.

"She seems a very lively girl," Old Jiang was the first to comment.

"Stands like an artist," added Aping.

"She's got a kind of dignity," concluded Hai Ping. His remarks were usually accurate. I gazed at Ren Jia anxiously. She sneered, "She looks too serious. Not sweet enough." How harsh she was! I wondered whether she was also as exacting with her students.

"Their sweets were the cheap kind, so they can't be well off." Old Jiang was always very sensitive about the question of prices, a result of his being hard up. I looked at him pityingly.

Having reached the ensemble's headquarters, I saw that the leaders were collecting money from everybody in order to buy presents for Xiao Ji and his bride. But the bridegroom was doing his utmost to stop them, declaring loudly that the reason why he hadn't breathed a word to anyone about his marriage was to save his colleagues spending their money. No one listened to him. It was a tradition that whenever anyone got married, we gave presents. It helped to make us feel like one big family.

I was chosen to give Xiao Ji the present from our group. Soon after supper, I went to his room.

The door was not locked. I heard the sound of hammering from inside, so I knocked several times. There was no response. I pushed open the door and stepped into the room. Xiao Ji was nailing up a picture; there were already several lying here and there on the floor. The bride was hanging one on the wall. Three walls were already full of them. They made the place look quite beautiful. Turning their heads at the same time, the newly-weds greeted me, "Welcome! Sit down, please!"

But the only stool in the room was being stood on by the bride, so I had to sit on the edge of their bed.

Putting down his hammer, Xiao Ji went to make tea for me, while his wife got down from the stool and hurried to bring me a dish of sweets. I looked around the room: only a table beside the bed, a kerosene stove, a pot and some enamelled bowls. With a dish of sweets in her hand, the bride came over to me, asking, "Does our room seem very shabby?"

Should I nod or shake my head?

"But, in fact, it isn't!" Pointing to the pictures she went on, "Look, we have magnolia, bamboos, mountains, river and the sun. . . ."

Smiling, I turned to Xiao Ji and reprimanded him, "Why don't you introduce her to me? I can't just call her 'bride'!"

Before he could open his mouth, his wife said, "Let me introduce myself. I'm Lian Zhu. I just graduated from the fine arts department of the Provincial Art College, I'm now working as a teacher in the First Middle School." She spoke the Beijing dialect with a strong provincial accent.

I then introduced myself, "I'm Songsong, one of the dancers."

"Were you an educated youth from Shanghai?"

I nodded my head. I gazed at her. The more I looked at her, the more I felt Ren Jia's remarks were unfair. In fact, she was very tender. It was just that she rarely smiled.

"I'm from the seaside."

I chuckled, drawn to her more and more. I realized from her accent that she came from the area around the port of Lianyun.

An outburst of noisy quarrelling interrupted us. Amazed, Lian Zhu stood up and walked towards the door. Xiao Ji and I followed her. I told her, "You'll get used to it after a week."

Opening the door, I spotted the shadow of someone moving towards us from the darkness and calling my name. It was Xiuwen! I remembered that, though she had been living here for more than a week, she was still curious about each quarrel. She would listen to it, inquire what it was all about and then spread the news.

"Xiao Zhang sent Old Jiang to buy half a catty of meat, but Old Jiang bought a whole catty. Now they're at each other's throats. Listen, it's getting worse. Let's go upstairs and try to patch things up between them!" Excitement glistened in her big eyes. I was immediately aware that what she suggested was not so much aimed at patching things up but at watching the fun. Feeling disgusted, I remarked indifferently, "No need. Let them sort it out themselves." Although they had quarrelled for more than six or seven years, even fiercely, they had no wish to divorce.

Lian Zhu agreed. "No couples want outsiders to interfere. Everyone has some self-respect."

Turning her face to the bride, Xiuwen looked her up and down. She urged, "Let's go and have a look at their room." Grabbing me by the hand, she dragged me there.

All of a sudden, there emerged before my eyes her room and furnishings. I tried to hold her back, but she had already rushed inside and stood in the centre of the almost empty room. She winked at me. Fearing that she might blurt out heaven knows what kind of criticism, I hastened to divert her attention.

"Are you going to watch television tonight?" I asked.

"Television?" She gazed at the bed on which lay two thin, old quilts, replying vaguely, "It's silly to look at TV every night."

"What about listening to your cassette tapes?"

"You can't listen to the same music over and over again."

"Where's Huang Jian?" I uttered the name I was unwilling to mention.

"Gone out to have fun," Xiuwen answered unhappily.

As it happened, Huang Jian's voice sounded in the yard, "Xiuwen! Xiuwen!"

"He's come back. Go home quickly!" I pushed her, relieved that she would have to leave. She moved towards the door slowly, saying, "We've nothing to talk about."

Finally she left the room, and the noise of the quarrel in the upstairs room also died away.

Looking up, Lian Zhu inquired in a soft voice, "Do they always quarrel?"

"Yes. They're often short of money."

"Really?" Turning around, she stared at me and then at Xiao Ji. In spite of her thick lenses, I could still see the look of doubt in her eyes. That was natural. Newly-weds only thought about love. Love. . . . How had they fallen in love? I couldn't restrain my curiosity and asked them.

The corner of Lian Zhu's mouth moved slightly, until she gave a rare yet moving smile. She gazed at her husband, who smiled back at her. Who would have ever noticed that this silent young carpenter had eyes like deep pools?

"How we fell in love? Where to begin? . . ." Lian Zhu felt embarrassed.

"Say whatever you like," her husband encouraged her.

"Oh, it's very simple," Lian Zhu began at last.

"No, it's very complicated in fact," the young man countered.

"We waited and waited. Shortly after we had been transferred here from the countryside, I went to study at college. He had to wait again until my graduation. It was always wait, wait. What about you?" Having nothing more to say, Lian Zhu launched into a counter-attack.

"Oh, we're an old married couple now."

"Nonsense! You're the same age as I. Twenty-nine, right?"

"Twenty-eight. It was really nothing special. He just kept pestering me with poems and music."

"And you didn't chase after him?"

"No, of course not!"

"What?" Lian Zhu seemed sorry.

"Didn't you also send him a poem?" Xiao Ji suddenly put in.

"How do you know that?" I cried out.

"Oh my dear Songsong!" Putting her arms round me, Lian Zhu giggled and soon I did too.

I sat there till after ten o'clock, then happily said good night. As soon as I reached my room, my joy evaporated. Aping told me that the leader of our ensemble had just telephoned him to say that rehearsals would begin tomorrow and we would go on tour again the following Monday. I refused at once. "I won't go!"

Putting down his pen, Aping stood up and reached out his hand to console me. I pushed him aside, walking towards the bed. "I won't go! Why should we go again? We only came back two weeks ago! I won't go!" I threw myself face down on the bed. To go on tour meant packing in a hurry, loading and unloading our luggage, setting cold stages and living together in a big room with many of our colleagues.... I was on the verge of tears.

Coming over to me, Aping embraced me and said

comfortingly, "I'll be there to help you. . . . Fill your hot water bottle."

"Is that all you can say?" I yelled angrily.

"What else do you want me to do?"

"I want you to get me transferred to another job. I don't want to dance any longer. I need a stable life, a settled home. I want . . . I want a baby!" The tears ran down my cheeks. Xiuwen's comfortable room appeared before my eyes. Ah, how much I wanted. . . .

Upset, Aping stroked my hair awkwardly.

3

In order to leave according to schedule, we had to work overtime. It was already very late at night when we returned home. In silence, we squeezed into the former janitor's room to leave our bicycles. After that, without saying good night to each other, we all hurried to our respective rooms. Most of our colleagues had some hot soup and warm rice ready, whereas Aping and I. . . . How I longed for some hot soup! Aping held my hands tenderly. Though I had worn two pairs of gloves, my hands were still cold. He put them into the pockets of his overcoat. I drew them out at once. I didn't want such tenderness. What I needed badly was a stable family life, not embraces and kisses!

I stopped involuntarily in front of Xiuwen's window, through which the apple-green light dimly shone. How cosy to be bathed in such a mild light. What was Xiuwen doing at this moment?

Several voices whispered below the window-sill — Old Jiang's three boys.

"Doesn't Aunty Li like to watch TV?" It was Old Jiang's youngest son, only three years old, speaking in a childish treble.

"Why doesn't she like to watch TV?"

Xiuwen's silhouette could be seen at the window; the soft light made her face more graceful and charming. I unconsciously touched my own cheeks. Because of the weather and stage make-up, my skin had become coarser.

The door was suddenly pushed open and Huang Jian came out. On seeing me, he smiled unexpectedly. Why did he smile at me? Was it because he no longer hated me? Or was he mocking my refusing him in the past? My heart ached. I wanted to get away, but my feet wouldn't move.

"Let's go," Aping said, biting his lips. His deep eyes flashed. He looked unwell. I started to move.

As soon as we reached our room, I threw myself on the bed, wanting to lie there for ever. But, my stomach was rumbling with hunger! Aping had bought me two stuffed steamed buns from our canteen, but, as I was angry with him, I had disdained to even look at them. I hadn't eaten anything for nine hours. I got up from the bed, took a bowl of cold rice and filled it with some hot water. Just as I was about to eat, Aping snatched it away from me. "Why let yourself get run down?"

"I'm hungry!" I shouted, stretching out my hand to grab the bowl.

"Don't you see that I've already begun to cook a meal!" Having put aside the bowl, he continued to cut up the cabbage.

"I can't wait!" I stamped my feet irritably.

"Have a biscuit then." Putting down the knife once more, he handed me a tin of biscuits.

"They're too dry. I don't want them! I won't eat them!" I pushed away the tin. It slipped from his fingers to the floor.

"You just want to pick a quarrel," his lips trembled.

"Who wants to pick a quarrel? I. . . ."

"It's you!" he interrupted me roughly. "You . . . you regret you made a wrong decision. If you had married him, you could also have become a wealthy lady and led a comfortable life!"

"You!" I was speechless with rage and shock.

Flushed with fury, he continued, "What were you thinking? I told you clearly I had no money, position or ability. I said you'd suffer if you married me! I warned you, didn't I? I was afraid all along you'd regret it. And as I expected, you have!"

Knowing not why, I suddenly slapped his face. Turning around, I flung myself on to the bed, sobbing. After a time, I fell asleep. When I woke up, I discovered I was lying under my cotton quilt, a hot water bottle at my side. The room was empty. Where was Aping? Where had he gone so late?

I felt I was suffocating as if there was some heavy weight on my chest. I was very hurt. How could he say such things to me? I had suffered so much by marrying him, yet he said that I regretted it. If I had taken a lift in Huang Jian's jeep that night, then I would . . . but, instead, I had chosen to hitch a ride on the rack of Aping's bicycle. Why had I done it? I was thinking that he could always play the piano at dancing practice; that he could conduct the orchestra to follow the steps of my solos. I was thinking of the endless stories he told me about Beethoven and Tchaikovsky. On account of this, my parents became angry with me, as did Director Huang of our Cultural Bureau. . . . Now Aping said that I. . . . Tears again ran down my cheeks. Had I ever regretted it? Did I envy Xiuwen for her good luck? No, I had never envied her. On the contrary, I looked down on her. She was so cheap. When Huang Jian declared his love for her, she immediately accepted him. All the young girls looked at her with disdain.

My watch had stopped. I didn't know what time it was, but I was sure it was very late. There was not the slightest sound in the courtyard. Suddenly the noise of a car engine broke the silence. Huang Jian stepped out from the car. He went out almost every night, leaving Xiuwen alone. How strange when they had such a comfortable room! Why was he unwilling to stay at home and sit and talk with his wife? How we longed to sit carefree at home and chat about things. But we had neither a comfortable room nor the time to talk.

The car headlights were finally switched off. Huang Jian entered his room and silence reigned again. Where was Aping? Why had I been in such a foul temper? I began to worry about him. Putting on my cotton-padded coat, I quickly got up and opened the door. I hurried along the passage formed by the sets. Almost every room was dark except Xiao Ji's where a lamp still shone brightly from the window. There were also faint sounds of voices. A pair of young lovers had, of course, a lot of things to talk about.

The gate of the courtyard was pushed open lightly, and a slender figure slipped in. He had come back finally. Unwilling to let Aping discover that I was waiting for him, I rushed back home.

Just as I got under my quilt, he stepped into the room. He came over to the bed. I pretended to have fallen asleep, but my eyelids moved. Then, he sat down at the table, holding his head in his hands. The bowl of cold rice and slices of half-cut cabbage remained on the table. So he hadn't eaten his supper. Where had he been?

4

It was Sunday the next day. After breakfast, Aping went out immediately with some music scores under his arm. I didn't ask him where he was going, for I was still angry with him. I didn't care a fig for him!

It was a fine day without a cloud in the blue sky. The sun shone warmly, making our small courtyard, which was usually crowded and untidy, appear large and bright. The yard was criss-crossed with clothes-lines, from which were hanging cotton-padded quilts and mattresses. A group of kids were playing hide-and-seek among them. Old Jiang's three sons were shouting at the tops of their voices. I brought out my trunk to air our clothes in the sunshine. Generally speaking, the climate in the north was very dry, yet, as we had been on tour for two months, our clothes could get musty.

Xiuwen was also busying herself airing their clothes. I saw that they had a lot: overcoats long, medium and short, of wool or other material. Xiuwen loved dressing elegantly. She never wore trousers which hadn't been well-pressed and shoes that were not well shined. In previous years, owing to financial difficulties, she had not been able to indulge herself. Now she could have anything she wanted. All of a sudden, she bent down and started to vomit. I ran over and held her arm, "Are you sick?" I asked. She nodded. "Does Huang Jian know?" I glanced at their room, but there was no sign of him.

"Yes, he knows. He bought me some medicine."

"Oh," I said no more. It would have been better if he could have kept her company more often.

I left Xiuwen and went back. At this moment, I saw that Lian Zhu was also busy with her clothes. In her trunk, apart from clothes, there were several parcels wrapped up in newspaper.

"What treasures have you hidden there?" I pointed at the parcels in the trunk.

"Letters," Lian Zhu answered in all seriousness.

"Letters?" I was at a loss. Picking up one, I saw on the newspaper was written: From the municipal ensemble to Sanpu Commune, 1975.

"That year, Xiao Ji had been transferred to work in your ensemble and I was still living and working in Sanpu Commune," explained Lian Zhu.

Another parcel was marked: From the Provincial Art College to the municipal ensemble, 1977.

"Those were the letters we wrote while I was studying."

One had only "Sanpu, 1970" written on it.

"They were the letters we wrote when we were both living in the same village." Smiling for a while, she took the parcel from my hand and laid it in a corner on which the sun shone directly. From her expression, I could guess that she treasured those letters the most.

Counting them, I found there were ten parcels altogether. So they had written to each other for ten years!

I exclaimed in surprise, "You were friends for ten years?"

"Yes."

"How was it in those years?"

She straightened her back, and said as if to herself, "Every day we ate coarse food and worked hard from early morning. But we managed because we had each other."

"It wasn't easy!" I sighed.

"Of course there were difficulties. You know the kinds of problems educated youths had when they fell in love."

"Yes, I know."

"If one was transferred to work in the city, the other had to wait. We waited years. At first, I feared I'd be a burden to him. Later on, when I entered college, he feared I'd refuse him." She smiled ironically. "We were always doubting."

"Did you ever waver?"

She shook her head slightly. "It wasn't easy, finding each other. We shared good and bad times. It would be unthinkable to start all over again with someone else."

Hearing this, I felt an ache in my heart.

"What if, in the future, well ... when you have some difficulty again, and this difficulty is quite different from ones in the past. Perhaps just an everyday problem, that is to say. . . ." I muttered, striving to find suitable words. "For example, just like Old Jiang and his wife, who quarrel over a few cents. Of course, it's ridiculous, but if you are really short of money, then. . . ."

"Oh, I see," she said, putting one hand on my shoulder and stretching out the other to twist a strand of my hair. She gazed up at the sky. "Material life is also very important to us. I can't be sure that we wouldn't quarrel or grumble over money. Still we can always remember what we went through together. Then I think we can probably manage to get over such problems."

I bent down my head, avoiding her eyes. Like them, Aping and I had also found each other and faced life's troubles together.

Lian Zhu continued, "It seems ages ago now, but it will always mean something to us because... because that's love. Without our love, we might have become depressed or lost hope during those years. But how can I preach to you old married couples! I'm determined to protect our love, to cherish our marriage. But that's not so easy to do."

For us, it was also not so easy. I sighed sadly.

"Why the sigh? Would you like to have lunch with us today?" she inquired, looking at me attentively.

I nodded my head.

The meal was very simple, but I ate quite a lot, probably because I hadn't eaten the night before. I noticed that most of the pictures on the walls had been put into frames. Not every family could possess such riches. With many things to prepare for the coming tour, we parted after lunch.

Aping still had not come home. Where was he? When would he return? I felt miserable because he hadn't eaten for a whole day. I hastened to prepare a meal for him. Having washed some onions, I sliced them and then broke some eggs. I'd cook rice with fried eggs. Before I had finished, Lian Zhu called me to go out with her.

Xiao Ji and Lian Zhu argued over every purchase. It was evening before we finished shopping.

It was already dark. The street lights lit up either side of the river and shone on its surface. While we were walking slowly along the bank, Lian Zhu remembered her home town. "How beautiful it was with blue waves, golden sun, shells, sandy beaches and sea-gulls. Standing on the shore, I felt I owned that vast world. Our life was so beautiful and we were so deeply in love. So we're not poor at all."

"We're only short of money," Xiao Ji added drily. We all laughed.

Back in our courtyard, the news on the radio reminded us it was already seven o'clock. Xiuwen was washing clothes and waved as soon as she saw us. When we went over to her, she asked Lian Zhu in a low voice, "Did you chat to Hai Ping yesterday?"

"Hai Ping?" Lian Zhu looked baffled, first at me then at her.

"That tall man with wavy hair."

"Ah, you mean that handsome one? Yes, we talked a bit while I washed clothes here yesterday."

"Good heavens! He and his wife have just had a fight about it. Didn't you know his wife's very jealous?"

"That's ridiculous!" Xiao Ji said angrily and pulled Lian Zhu away with him.

Opening her mouth awkwardly, Xiuwen didn't know what to do. I felt sorry for her. To smooth things over, I said casually, "So we'll be off again soon. How I envy you!"

She forced a smile. Xiao Ji had embarrassed her. She bent down to pick up the wooden tub, but couldn't lift it. I realized that she was pregnant and asked, "Where's Huang Jian? Why doesn't he give you a hand?"

"He's bought a washing machine for me, but it hasn't been connected yet. It can't be used for the time being."

I helped her to carry the tub to her room. Huang Jian had money; he could buy a lot of things. But money can't buy everything. At her door, I put down the tub and was about to leave, when she said suddenly, "When you go away I'll feel lonely again."

"Then don't let Huang Jian gad about so much. You must make him stay at home with you."

"We don't seem to have much to say to each other." She had expressed this many times, but now she seemed depressed. I wondered whether she had been upset by the unpleasant scene or whether, because I had only admired her, I hadn't noticed her unhappiness before.

How to comfort her? Huang Jian and she had fallen in love with each other at first sight. Perhaps it had been a bit too easy. They had never experienced any difficulties. Their romance had been quite smooth. After a while, I said, "No, you won't feel lonely. You have your TV set, tape-recorder and. . . ."

"I'm tired of them," she shook her head.

The gate of the courtyard was suddenly pushed open for a car. Huang Jian threw out a parcel which Xiuwen caught. She quickly unwrapped it and found a new short jacket in the latest fashion. With a cry of joy, she left me and rushed into her room to try it on. This would keep her amused for the moment. When she grew tired of it, Huang Jian would buy her a new one. But what if he could no longer produce something new or she tired too quickly of his presents? What would happen then? The apple-green light could not be a substitute for love.

This made me long for Aping. What was he doing? I went home, but there was no light on and the door was locked. When I went in I saw the onion slices and bowl of eggs untouched on the table. Where had he gone? I got on my bike and rode along the main street.

Where could I find him? First of all, I went to our new building. Perhaps he was practising there. But there was no sign of him. Then, I headed for the municipal cultural centre, in case he was chatting to his buddies. But it was in darkness. Then I thought of his students. I hurried to their houses. He hadn't been to the first two I called on, so I went to the third one. This was the home of Doctor Chang, who worked at the municipal hospital. His daughter was taking piano lessons from Aping. Doctor Chang told me that Aping had just left there an hour ago and that he had already signed a sick-leave certificate for me, which Aping had taken. I was at a loss to understand. Doctor Chang said, "He came yesterday evening and said he desperately needed it. This morning he came again to urge me to write it, so I promised to give him it this evening. I gave it to him, because he never asked any favour from me before." So that was it! I left without a word. Racing home, I nearly knocked down some pedestrians. How impatient I was to find Aping!

Riding over the Huoping Bridge, I saw a familiar figure standing under a street lamp. Aping! The dim light cast a faint shadow on the ground. With both hands, he was holding the railing looking at the river. What was he thinking about? I wanted to call him, but I was too excited to utter a sound. Putting down my bike, I ran over to him.

On hearing my steps, he turned his face, stared at me silently and produced a sheet of paper from his breast pocket. I took it, folded it and slowly tore it into pieces.

"What's wrong with you?" he asked in a daze.

"Nothing." Tears ran down my cheeks.

"What's the matter?" He removed the pieces from my hands.

"If I remain here, how can you manage?" Sobbing, I grabbed the pieces again and threw them into the river.

With his eyes shining brightly, Aping embraced me tenderly.

"What were you thinking about here?" I asked him in a soft voice.

"I was thinking about how we stood here the first time. Do you still remember? It was precisely here that I told you, 'I love you!' I'd been in agonies for ages, afraid that you'd reject me. It was clear that you could lead a more comfortable life if. . . ."

I covered his mouth with my hand, but he took it away and continued, "But you said you loved me and told me, 'I only want you. I want no one else but you!' "

5

It was time to set off again. The leader of our ensemble decided to arrange for the bus to pass by our court-yard. Early in the morning, we gathered together in the yard to wait for its arrival and say goodbye to our families.

The parting conversation between Old Jiang and his wife was filled as usual with calculations.

"Post me twenty yuan next month."

"I'll post you thirty."

"Nobody asked you to send so much," snapped his wife, ignoring her husband's kindness.

"You'd better pay more attention to your meals during the tour."

"I'll post you thirty."

"No, I need only twenty."

. . . . . .

I couldn't refrain from laughing. They still loved each other. They were only short of money.

Ren Jia and Hai Ping stood face to face. Ren Jia fixed her eyes full of worry and fear on Hai Ping. Hai Ping said something to her, which I couldn't hear distinctly, probably to set her mind at ease. To tell the truth, apart from his being handsome, there was nothing to give her cause to doubt him. It was not easy for Hai Ping to endure the jealousy of his plain, narrow-minded wife. If he didn't love her, then why did he suffer so? Yet she was too anxious to keep his love to herself. She simply wouldn't share even a tiny bit.

Xiao Ji and Lian Zhu hadn't appeared yet, and the cause was obvious. They had so often been apart before and now they were to be separated again. Xiao Ji was unable to find himself a comfortable job. How long would they have to write letters to each other?

All of a sudden, I felt very happy. At least Aping and I were always together. I turned to look at Aping. He held my hands tightly. As usual they were as cold as ice. He put my hands into his deep overcoat pocket.

It was very warm because he had put a hot water bottle in it. What a silly, dear fellow!

The bus arrived. After we had all stowed our luggage on the racks and sat down, I noticed the apple-green light was still shining in Xiuwen's home, pale in the dawn. Huang Jian was gazing at me from the window. Before he could do anything, I smiled at him.

The bus was carefully driven out of the gate. Our small courtyard was not so poor after all.

Translated by Hu Zhihui